RAMBLIN'
LI
AND NOW THE REST OF THE STORY

Cider Dan

THIS IS MY LIFE STORY

AS I REMEMBER IT

THIS IS A TRUE STORY

By Cider Dan

Edited by Don Rickerson

Ramblings of a Wore Out Lumber Jack

Book 2

And Now the Rest of the Story

CIDER DAN

THIS IS MY LIFE STORY

AS I REMEMBER IT

THIS IS A TRUE STORY

First printed 2002, Reprinted by permission 2022

Edited by Don Rickerson

RickersonDon@gmail.com

All rights reserved

Copyright ©2022

ISBN 978-1-6781-8462-9

Cover photo by permission of

3 Broke Girls Gallery, Corry PA

Contents

Foreword iv
Chapter 1 1
Chapter 2 9
Chapter 3 15
Chapter 4 16
Chapter 5 19
Chapter 6 20
Chapter 7 23
Chapter 8 25
Chapter 9 28
Chapter 10 33
Chapter 11 34
Chapter 12 36
Chapter 13 37
Chapter 14 38
Chapter 15 43
Chapter 16 45
Chapter 17 47
Chapter 18 54
Chapter 19 57
Chapter 20 59
Chapter 21 61
Chapter 22 63
Chapter 23 67
Chapter 25 74
Chapter 26 78
Index of Names 81

Foreword

What a pleasure it has been to work on the two Cider Dan books, giving us a glimpse into Amish life in Northwestern Pennsylvania.

I would like to thank "Whitey" Byler, Cider Dan's son for permission to reproduce the book and help with the editing and Rick Neylon for facilitating the work with Whitey.

To help understand the book a bit better, I would like to define a couple of items.

First Amish name conventions: when they refer to another Amish person in the familiar case, they use the father's name and then the child's name. For example, Dan Byler's son Whitey would be called "Dan's Whitey." This is because Amish families are very large, so you could have 100 cousins all with the same last name, so referring the child to the father helps better define someone.

A married couple, in the familiar case, is referred to using the husband's first name and the wife's first name. So, Mr. Dan Byler and Mrs. Mattie Byler would be referred to as Dan-Mattie.

Second, the lumberjack jobs in a sawmill. The Sawyer is the guy running the cutting machine that cuts boards from a log. The Off-Bearer is the guy who removes the cut piece when it drops from the saw. The Edger is the one who cuts or prepares to cut the sides from the board. The Grader is the one who determines the quality of the board. The Piler is the person(s) who receive the cut board and stack it into drying piles.

Don Rickerson

Chapter 1

I will try and write another book as people say I left too much out of my other book Will start when we were boys. Us four oldest ones swiped two bottles of Dad's homebrew and headed for the barn. I was probably 9 or 10 years old, and the other boys were younger. I kept telling the other boys I can drink more than they can as I am older and bigger. I don't remember how much of those two bottles we drank but we were all stretched out. And did we have a mad Dad and Mother!

I remember one time Mother got mad at Bim. There was an old apple orchard across the driveway, all weeds and brush. Well, little Bim tried to run away and Mom right after him. Well, Mom caught him. She beat him and kicked him and really worked him over; he looked a little like Beetle Baily when Sarge gets done with him. But I still don't think Bim got the lickings us other boys got.

When I was sixteen years old, my little mother beat me once. Me and Monty's Bill were down at Freeman Yoder's and we were drinking a little cider. Before I knew it, I must have had a little too much. I got to go home, and I didn't seem too steady on my feet. Well, I started up Bundysburg Hill. We lived on the other side of Lester Yoder. Uncle Ben's lived next to the railroad track where Steve Byler owned.

Well, all at once I started getting a bellyache. Boy, did I have a bellyache. I thought I could make it to Uncle Ben's. Inside the barn door was Ben's buggy and there was a workbench there, too. But there was always room to get between the buggy and the workbench.

I made it through the door, and it was a little dark in there. I was really in a hurry when I went between Ben's buggy and that workbench when CRASH! Everything let loose. It was all over and what a mess.

Steve was there that day and piled some shingles in that alleyway and that was what I fell over. Well, I made it home and my mother beat me and kicked me. There was an old shanty out back and that's where I woke up the next morning. I snuck in the house, nobody was up yet and got some clean clothes. I was in Swine Creek swimming when the sun came up.

Wally was down at Freeman's one-night drinking cider and when he got home, he walked right into one of those big maple trees and fell flat on his butt.

He looked up at Freeman and said, "Freeman, I didn't know that tree was there."

Freeman said, "Wally, that tree has been there for a hundred years."

Back in those days us young guys had all the answers. But now since I'm older I haven't got any answers. In still trying to get over my cancer surgery and my radiation treatments and it's pretty rough. I have a lot of time to think.

Today, 36 years ago, Aug. 9, 1967, we moved to Sparty. I've learned a lot of dos and don'ts in all these years.

Aug. 11- Joe Kurtz and wife, Joe's son Aul and wife, Yogi and wife Maryann and Bishop Jake Kaufman were here all afternoon. The afternoon was way too short. We were together a lot when we were young, we worked together. Now we hardly see each other anymore.

You know, when you've had cancer and have been all cut up, and then they find a spot on your lung and they don't know what it is, and you have to wait and see what it does, you have some days when you feel pretty rough. I have no voice box, but I can talk if I put my thumb over that hole in my throat. Croak would be a better word, but people can understand me pretty good.

Then you get a day when some of your old buddies come to see you. It's better than medicine.

I had my sawmill up in Geneva on the lake for four years before I moved to Sparty. Joe Kurtz skidded logs with mules and we agreed that it would probably be better if a man that has religion wouldn't own a mule. They say there are good mules and I think I saw one once. He laid on his back, four legs sticking straight up in the air and he wasn't breathing! No, just kidding. There are good mules. But most of the good ones are in Eastern PA.

When we worked up in Geneva, Ohio, Joe Kurtz got a red mule off of old Sawmill Dan. He wanted to pay for him, but old Dan said no, you take that mule and try him out first. Well, Joe hauled that red mule up to Geneva and took him back to the barn. They just slapped a horse barn up about 50 foot from the mill.

Joe named him Clarence. Well, Clarence was a little thin and Joe decided to feed him awhile. So, he hooked his other mules up and headed for the woods I started sawing and the first thing I knew the slabs and boards started flying and he ripped loose and kicked the side out of the barn and down through the woods he went. Well brother Andy was cutting logs and they finally caught him and brought him back to the barn. They tied him up good and fixed the barn again. It wasn't long the boards and slabs were flying again and away went old Clarence again. Well, Joe's blood pressure was pretty high and still rising. We finally caught old Clarence again.

Joe said, "ribs or no ribs, old Clarence is going to skid logs." That's when the fun started. We went along out to the woods to watch the fun. Joe drove up to a log and stopped. He then loaded the log on the sled, picked up the lines, and said, "Giddyap."

Clarence backed up with his hind feet in the back of the second bunk. Then he went airborne. That sled took off with a jerk and the log stayed where it was. We had a merry old time with Clarence, but Joe got him going and started skidding logs. But he didn't enjoy working with that mule. He took the little mule home.

One Friday night, Joe told my brother Andy," I'm going to hook that little mule in the buggy and drive to Liddlefield. "

Andy said," I will go along." They hooked that little mule in the buggy and Joe had his mule prod.

You can't whip a mule, you have to have a prod and poke him in the rear. They got to Middlefield and people were walking on the sidewalk and Joe didn't dare use his prod. That little mule walked real slow. Joe said they had traffic backed up for quite a ways but they finally got to the parking lot. When they had the shopping done it was dark.

Brother Andy said, "I think I'll get a taxi to go home."

Joe said, "Well, why?"

Andy said "That mule hasn't been driven after dark. What is she going to do when two headlights start to come at her, probably, he will go right between them."

Joe said," Naw, she won't do anything."

So, they headed out Rt. 87 for home. She went real good, car lights didn't bother her. All at once a buggy started to pass them and Joe started using his prod again and put that little mule in the galop and the race was on. That buggy didn't pass them. They went the galop the whole way home. A mule, when he is going the gallop wide open, his hind feet almost clip his ears. I'm still glad I wasn't on that buggy.

Anyway, we ran out of timber and had to move the mill. Everything was going good till we hooked Clarence and the other mule to the GM sawmill motor. They walked off with it at first. Then Clarence threw one of his fits. Joe told him to go, and he put it in reverse and backed into the radiator. Joe got them straightened up again and told them to go and kerbang! into the radiator again. I hollered whoa, he's going to bust my radiator off. Brother Andy grabbed a 1 by 6 by 8 and a hand full of 8 penny nails and pounded them into the end of the board. Andy held the board up by the radiator and Joe told Clarence to go. Bang, he backed right into those nails and stood there and rubbed his hind end on those nails. Joe hollered for Rufus to bring his team over and a log chain. They hooked the log chain around Clarence's neck and hooked the other team on the claw. Rufus told his team to go. They took off towing Clarence. He had all four feet sliding but he went. They went through a mud hole and Clarence flopped on his side and, bang, he was up again.

So, Joe finally gave up on him. One night he hired a truck and took Clarence home and put him in the barn.

He went in and told Sawmill Dan, "I brought your mule home."

Dan said, "I've been expecting him."

I never heard any more about Clarence and I didn't ask any questions.

That reminds me of another mule story. When my brother Smiley had his mill out here, I cut logs and Pinky skidded logs. One was Chubby Dan's mule and I don't remember who the other mule belonged to. There was a ditch went down through the woods and it was full of water. So we cut a bunch of poles and threw them in the ditch. Well, Pinky crossed that ditch for several days. Then one day I heard him holler and he kept on hollering, so I went running up there. Well, Chubby's mule laid in the ditch full of water and Pinky was holding her nose out of the water with the line.

He said, "she's gonna drown."

I said, "Pinky, hold her nose under the water not out. She'll lay there all day if you hold her nose out of the water. That's a lot easier than skidding logs."

I took the line from him and put my foot on her nose and held it under the water

Pinky said, "if she drowns, you're going to pay for her."

I said she's not gonna drown." Pretty soon the bubbles came up and I said, "give her room, she's gonna get up. And bang, she was on her feet. That was about the first mule lesson Pinky had and also one of the last. If I remember right, he quit shortly after that.

We were working just down the road from my place and the Chubby mule was about too lazy to breathe. One day Pinky had a little glass jar of fruit in his dinner bucket. That night at quitting time he hung his dinner bucket on this chubby mule's hame. He started up the road standing on the back bunk of the sled when this jar started rattling on this dead headed mule's hames. Well, I'll tell you what, you talk about 2 mules waking up, they woke up. One second they were going at a slow walk and the next second they were wide open with Pinky standing on the back bunk hanging on for dear life. They made it in the driveway, I don't know-how, the speed they were going, but they did. When I got up to the barn Pinky was mad. If I remember right that was when he quit. He told me he's hard up but he doesn't have to work with something like that. I think that was the end of Pinky's mule days.

I remember one time my brother Andy went and bought a mule team to skid logs. I don't remember who was skidding for him at the time. I think it was the first day whoever was skidding came into the mill and said the one mule laid down and won't get up. So, they all went out to the woods and tried and tried to get that mule up, but they couldn't get him up. So, Andy went back to the mill and brought the high lift out and ran the forks under him real easy and slowly picked him up and set him on his feet. Then he slowly started lowering his forks, but every time the mule got a little weight on his legs, they would just buckle. Finally, Andy got sick of it and just dropped him and told the crew, let's go get something we can skid logs with. They took the other mule and headed for the barn and before they got there here came the other mule the gallop. He didn't want to miss out on his grain. So, brother Andy went mule hunting again.

Lit Dan's Jerry and his brother Mel had some experience with mules. They were working on a sawmill, I don't know whose mill it was but there was an Al J. Miller was off-bearing. Either Jerry or Mel were skidding logs and must be this one mule was giving them trouble. I don't know the details of what was happening that forenoon, but Jerry and Mel must not have been very nice to this mule.

At dinner time Al said, "I've been watching you and I've been wondering how you two would take it if I treated you like you are treating those mules.

Either Jerry or Mel asked, "Do you want to skid logs this afternoon? "

and Al said," Yes, I would."

Al must not have known what makes a flippen mule tick. Well, after dinner, he headed for the woods. I don't know if it was the first or the second load the mill ran out of logs. So, the sawyer and the off bearer walked out to the woods to see how Al was making out. When they got out there, Al's blood pressure must have been about 290/148. They said Al had this mule by the top lip with one hand and by the bottom lip with the other hand and he hung on that mule's lips with all his weight.

You know, I don't think I know this man, but I would like to shake his hand. I know the feeling. I owned two teams of mules myself and I had one good one out of four. And she wasn't anything to brag about. Too big for light work and too light for heavy work. She had one bad habit. When you'd open that barn door in the morning, she'd go bang, bang, bang with her front foot against the manger. She wouldn't quit till she had her grain. Well, I wasn't too fond of that mule anyhow and I decided a mule wasn't going to rule me, so I started when I'd get in the barn in the morning, I had twine ready, and I'd tie her front feet together. Then I'd feed the cows and take my good old time before I'd feed the mules. I did this for quite a while and finally, I thought she'd quit. So, the next morning I didn't tie her feet together and there it goes again. She would not quit till she had her grain.

I just have to put this in this book about Rufus and my brother Bim. This happened when we were working up in Geneva, Ohio.

I talked to brother Bim about a month ago and he asked me, "are you writing another book?"

I said," I sure am."

He said, "I wish you'd keep the lies out of this one. "

I said," All the things I wrote about you were true, and what I write about you in this book will be true."

If I remember right, when we'd move mill, the log skidder and the lumber skidder would put up a barn with slabs and old lumber, then when we'd move mill again the barns would stay there. Well, Rufus had a little barn for his team of horses. Bim always was a little lazy. (Now he's going to call that a lie.) But I'll prove it to you. Instead of going to the brush, he started crapping in Rufus 'barn. Rufus warned him a couple of times then he'd quit. Pretty soon he'd start again. Well, one day when Rufus came in for dinner, Bim was already sitting there eating his dinner.

Rufus walked over and grabbed Bim around the neck and started dragging him over to the horse barn. Of course, we jumped up and went along to watch the fun. Well, Rufus got Bim into the horse barn. Boy, for a little guy, there was a pretty good-sized pile of poop there in the middle of the floor. Rufus drug Bim over to it. He had Bim around the neck with his right arm and his left hand was flat on the floor. Bim had a hold of Rufus 'right arm with his right arm and he had Rufus by the wrist with his left hand. They started going down and it looked like Rufus was gonna get it done. I thought, now look, little Bim is my baby brother, and I don't want to stand here and watch this. But I decided he was warned a couple of times and if Rufus was man enough to handle a cider; so be it.

Well, they kept going down further and further and finally it was close enough that Bim had to do something or be talked about for a long time afterward. I think it was getting to the point where things weren't smelling too good to little Bim. All at once Bim yanked on Rufus' left hand and it was so quick it worked. He picked Rufus' hand off the floor, and PLOP right in the middle of that pile. Rufus was so surprised his arms opened right up and Bim took off. I don't know how high Rufus' blood pressure went, but the bad part of t was, it didn't come down right away. Bim stayed out of his way for quite a while and finally things got back to normal.

Chapter 2

I worked on a sawmill all my life. I had a few cows for quite a few years off and on and some of this stuff I have to write down when I remember it. This is something that happened quite a few years ago.

Manas Troyer's Roy and Fred Barstow were working together on a sawmill Roy was sawing and Fred was running the edger. The sawmill was set up on top of a gully. When they had to go to the bathroom, they had to go down over the bank. There was little brush growing on the bank. One day Roy had to go, and he ran down over the bank and he was in a hurry. Well, he just got started good and little Fred started rolling rocks down over the gully. Roy must have had quite a time dodging those rocks and doing what he went down there to do. But he finally made it and when he was done, he grabbed a short stick and stuck the end in his pile of do-do. He went up the bank, keeping his short stick hid from Fred.

Fred put the motor in gear and wound her up ready to go. Roy rolled a log on the carriage and dogged it and took off a slab then a board. Fred grabbed the board and flipped it over on the edger. Roy reeled over for another board and grabbed his short stick, while Fred had his back turned and rubbed the do-do end across the log and took off another board. Fred grabbed it and flipped it over and saw this brown streak on the board. He bent over and looked and looked and couldn't figure out what it was. Finally, he stuck his finger in it then he smelled his finger, then he knew what it was. They said Roy laughed so hard he rolled on the ground. I have to laugh just thinking about it.

We had seven boys and the Slab and Grab sawmill is where they got their education. The first couple of years I sawed myself. When Tobe got old enough, he wanted to saw so he started sawing, I think Noah ran the edger and I think Mary and Marty worked in the back of the edger. When the boys started piling lumber, I told them how I wanted it piled. Well, it didn't soak in and I kept telling them, and finally, I just got sick of it. One day I checked their cherry grade pile, and I tore the whole bundle apart and said, now pile it over again. Then they started piling lumber. The girls were the best pilers; Mary and Marty.

We sawed cherry for seven years for Bill Reese. Then he started to buy logs from another company, then we sawed everything. Bill's log scaler would scale the logs in our yard and he'd mark them veneer and the rejects and they'd have to go on a separate pile. They'd truck them over to Spartywood. Well, if I'd leave for an hour or two, the boys would jump on the lift and put a grab of these good logs on the skidway and saw them up. One day I went to Buell's Corner and was gone about an hour. I came back and there was one log left on the skidway and it was a nice log and had a bright red V on it for veneer. I told them to shut the mill down.

I said, "I don't know how I did this but don't tell anybody. I pulled it off and put it back in the veneer pile. I felt pretty bad about this then years later, when it was too late to kick rear ends, they told me the rest of the story.

We always shut the mill down at 3:30 as we always had chores. In the summer we had those bull-headed, miserable Jerseys. I still like a nice Jersey cow but getting them in stanchions sometimes was a job. That one night that one heifer didn't want to put her head in the stanchion. Well, when we finally got her in, I hauled off and hit her right between the eyes with my fist and I kept on doing chores. I grained the cows, and I thought my finger felt funny. When I had time to check it out, it was broke. It's still crooked. If that old barn could talk, it could tell some pretty good stories.

The first three cows I bought were a little black Jersey and two little boned Guernsey's. That little black Jersey was a good little cow, but about once a month, she'd wipe you out. Then she had to have her licking and she'd be alright for another month. She would milk 48 lbs. when she freshened and after about three months, she would drop back to 40 lbs. and there she would stay. A lot of our Jerseys were registered. Some of the smart alec Holstein farmers said, put a quarter in the bucket and if the milk covers the quarter, she's registered.

Well, anyhow, we had some good times and some that weren't so good. I bought a first calf heifer one time, and she wasn't worth 2¢. One night I was milking the cow next to her. It was in the summertime and I was milking away. I must have been leaning forward because all at once my back started to get wet and warm. I turned around and looked and that Jersey heifer had her rear end twisted over towards me and she done that on purpose. How everybody knows when cows are on grass their poop gets real thin. Well, this ran down my back, inside my pants. What a mess. Well, the cider kids got a laugh out of this. They laughed hard enough that we had Jersey steaks the next night for supper.

Now old AL's Mel, I think most of you people know who I mean. He farmed and he had one Jersey cow. He told me that first summer he took his hat off to milk. Well, she got pretty vicious with her tail. One night he jumped up and cut all the hair off her tail with his jack-knife, up to the bone. Now the old girl wouldn't switch him in the face anymore. So, things went along good for a while. He said one night he was milking her, and her tail went around about three times, and clunk, right on top of his bald head. Old Mel let that go and he said the next night, clunk, she did it again. He said she was doing it on purpose, and I believe it. A couple of nights later she did it again. Mel jumped up and hollered at the hired man. He said, go get me the hatchet and a block of wood. The hired man did, and Mel held the block of wood up to her tail and chopped it off. She had a stub about 8 or 9 inches long.

He said," There, old girl, how do 19 you like that."

Things went along pretty good for a while and one night when he went in beside her to set down and milk, as he was sitting down, she stuck that stub out sideways and stuck him right in the eye. That was the last straw for that Jersey as Mel called a truck and sent her to the sale.

Now Pinky was a Jersey man and one time he went and bought a Holstein that milked 80 lbs. That was the trouble with Pinky, he would do crazy things like that without asking me what I thought. The first milk check he got after he got her milk in the can, I went over to see him. He wasn't in too good a humor.

I said, "Well what was your test?" We were always trying to outdo each other on tests.

He looked at me and said," the way I'm thinking right now, the less that cow milks, the more money I'll make." So, he didn't have her long, she went down the road.

The seven years I worked for Glo Ray Inc. sawmill, I had Jersey cows. A man by the name of Larry Lincoln worked on the mill. Now Larry was a nice guy, he claimed he was a little related to Abe Lincoln. I don't know about that, but he was a nice guy, and he went to church. Jitter cut logs for Glo Ray and on rainy days him and Don, the skidder would work on the mill. One day we were sitting there eating dinner and we got to talking about kicking Jersey cows. Old Larry could tell some pretty good ones. I was telling them about a Jersey I had that kicked pretty bad. Then Larry started. He said his Dad had a Jersey cow one time that kicked so bad, she'd kick with both hind feet at the same time and hit both her horns at the same time. This was one of the days Jitter was working on the mill.

Pretty soon Jitter said," Larry, what is your preacher's name?"

Larry said, "Why do you want to know?"

Jitter said, "Because he's got some work to do on you, that's why."

We all got a good laugh out of that one, and Larry laughed right with us. One night one of the boys were milking and all at once that Jersey wiped him right out. I mean, he flew, the milk stool flew, and the bucket flew.

I said, "You boys still don't know how to milk a cow."

I grabbed the milk stool and the bucket, and I sat down and started to milk that old girl, and not very gently, either. I told the boys," Now, here's how you milk a cow."

I had no more than said it when crashy, bang, slam, that old girl wiped me out. The boys all had a sober look on their faces, but I knew what those boys were thinking. Well, I had to read the old girl from the book and a few other things, too. Then I sat down and finished milking her.

Pinky used to tell me that Jersey cows, mules, and Leghorn chickens go together. I had a little team of Belgium's, about 1400lbs apiece. They weren't a bad little team except one was willing to do it all and the other one was willing to let him. The boys knew about as much about farming as I did and that wasn't very much. One day I told Noah to take the team across the road and plow up a new garden spot. He went down one side and then went over about 100 feet and went down that side. The only thing wrong was, he threw the dirt in. That day that little team wanted to plow the gallop. The plow was throwing dirt about 10 feet sideways. Then somebody went past and saw what was happening and told Joe Cicatella down at the store. So, he jumped in his truck and came up and pretty soon we had a few spectators watching. Noah was mad. He said, "Dad, if we ever just farm for a living, we will starve!"

I think this is about the time the boys got to talking about a little sabotage. I think I was sawing at the Slab and Grab at the time. Noah was working in the back of the edger and we started hitting spikes. Now, these spikes looked fairly new to me. The boys still say I had a snarl on my face when I was sawing. Even my baby brother Bim says that. Well, anyway, the next spike I hit, I just looked at Noah. That made him mad. He felt I was blaming him. Well, I wanted him to know his name was on the list. The next couple of days we really hit spikes. I found out years later, when it was too late to give him a good whaling, he took a hand full of spikes and went out on the log pile that night and said, "if he's going to blame me, I'm gonna do it." And he pounded those spikes into the logs. But he made awful sure Dad couldn't prove it on him.

Well, about this time we got a phantom shitter over at the sawmill. Now the Slab and Grab was across the road from our house and barn. For a long time, there was a pile of crap in the back of the edger every morning, on the platform. And it wasn't dog crap, either. I tried my best to find out who it was and to this day I don't know. Nobody will own up to it. I was mad at my little team one day. If I remember right, it was a warm day in the fall. I had a sled load of sloppy cow manure on. In the back of the barn, there was a hump in the road. If the team kept going, you could stand on the back of the sled and keep your balance. I remember, I didn't have a coat on, bare arms, and for some reason, when that sled load of manure took a nosedive, that little team stopped. It threw me forward and my arms went into that sloppy manure up to my elbows. Well, I left the team stand and went into the barn for the water hose to clean up. The boys were real sober faced. But I knew when I went out of hearing how it would sound. Oh well, when you think back you get a laugh out of things like that, but at the time it wasn't fun.

Chapter 3

Some of this stuff I have to write down as I think of it. One winter day Guy Bimber took Lester Byler up on Long Road to Abe C. Miller. It was snowing and blowing pretty bad. When Bimber pulled into Abe's driveway, he got stuck.

Finally, Abe came out and said to Bimber, "I've got one mule. I don't know if he can pull you out, but I can hook him up and we can try it."

Bimber said, "I have a mule in here,"(he meant Lester), "let's hook them together."

Abe said, "All right, but let's mark them as I want mine back." Abe lived right in back of me when he died, and I still miss him. Abe C. and Cider Jake's Jakie were talking one day. Abe was telling how warm it gets in Kentucky.

Jakie said, "Well, people don't work when it gets that warm, do they?"

Abe said, "sure they do, Jakie, there aren't any ciders down there."

This ticked Jakie off.

Chapter 4

The days the Slab and Grab started running were the days we lived on deer meat and potatoes. My old 30-30 put a lot of meat on the table, a lot more than some people give me credit for. Then after Joe Cicatella bought the Buell's Gorner Store, we had our chuck hunts. One thing that started out kind of innocent back in those days. Mattie always had a nice garden. Then the old woodchucks started to help themselves. All she would have had to do is tell me about it, and I would have taken care of it. But no, she wanted to shoot them herself. Well, anyway, I taught her how to shoot a gun. She shot a couple of chucks, and then she couldn't hit them anymore.

I said, "Mom, you're doing something wrong. Are you keeping your eyes open?"

She said, "I only shut them when I pull the trigger."

If only I would have shut up then, but I didn't. I said, "you have to keep your eyes open when you shoot.

Well, that's when my troubles started. I had an old 22 I let her use, but I laid the law down that was the only gun she could use. I think everyone knows about the forbidden fruit. It was long after that, when I went to the Buell's Corner Store, people started asking me, well how many woodchucks have you shot this summer? Well, I hadn't gotten very many, and when I'd tell them, they'd get a little smirk on their face. About this time, I started to get a funny feeling. I got beat that summer and again the next summer. One day the next summer, we were sitting on the back porch after dinner.

I said, "Mom, out by the shop there's a big woodchuck. Stick the 22 out of the window and let him have it. "

I knew he was too far away for just a 22. I was sitting in my easy chair, then I saw the window open out of the corner of my eye. I saw the barrel come out of the window and I was all ready to laugh because I knew she'd never get it. All at once, KER- BOOH! It picked me right off my easy chair.

I said, "Mom, you're a crook."

She was using my pet chuck rifle and out by the shop laid a dead woodchuck. The gun was a Model 7 Rem. in a 223 cal. with a 12-power scope. Not an old women's gun by any means. I tried to explain to her that this wasn't the deal, but she wouldn't listen. Then sometimes I would come home from work and besides the driveway laid two woodchucks. Some of my own so-called hunting buddies dropped them off for her.

Now Joe Cicatella was the kind of guy, when we'd go chuck hunting, he'd almost do an autopsy on a chuck I shot before he let me count him. I remember one time I shot a chuck and she started crawling for her hole, which wasn't far, and she made it. Now we got up there, her intestines were scattered out on the ground, but the chuck was in her hole. Do you think Joe would let me count that chuck? No, he would not.

I said, "Joe, if the best surgeon in the country had her on the operating table, there would be no hopes for her, and you know it."

Before Joe would let me count a chuck, she had to be laying in front of him and she had better be dead. I think some of those chucks he would have liked to give mouth to mouth to keep me from counting them. Joe would also get me in trouble once in a while, like one night we were going chuck hunting and went past Cripple Billy's place. Well, out by the road, there was Billy Alma, bent over right next to the road with her back towards the road. We were just going, and Joe had his window rolled down. He reached into his shirt pocket and pulled out an M80 firecracker. We got to about the right place, I took my lighter and lit it. Then Joe pitched it behind Alma as we went by. Now, who do you think got the blame for that? No.1, it wasn't my firecracker, and No.2 I didn't through it. The little bit I did, shouldn't have counted. Joe had a lighter in his pocket so the firecracker would have got lit anyway. (I think I would have made a good defense lawyer.) Well, any way Alma had it coming.

Come to find out everything, I did feel kind of bad. Found out later, Alma had a can of kerosene in it and was getting Japanese beetles off her flowers. When that firecracker went off, Alma about came apart. She was soaked in kerosene. Made me feel kind of bad, then I happened to think of something. One time I was gonna build birdhouses in my little workshop. Well, Alma took a bunch of old boards and nailed them together. Nails sticking out all over, the most awful looking thing you ever saw. Then she hung it up in Buell's Store and put my name on it. That was the end of my birdhouse business. But me and Alma declared a truce now. We're buddies again, probably until this book comes out.

Chapter 5

Now my thoughts go back to when I was a kid. One summer we lived in three shanties in the woods right by a sawmill where Dad worked. I remember Mony's Andy sawed, but that's all I remember. There was another family lived there from W.V. They also lived in shanties I still remember their names, Ken and Freda Spencer. 0ne day Dad and Mom went somewhere and Freda came up and wanted to use Mom's washing machine to wash.

I said, "Sure, go ahead."

I even helped her carry the water up from the pond. Well, Freda washed her clothes. She had 5 or 6 kids and her wash was pretty dirty. When she got done, I thought it's a shame to waste all this water, so I went and got Mom's clothes and washed for Mom. I even hung them on the lines to dry. I didn't know anything about sorting the white clothes, so they all got washed together. That was one of the biggest surprises I think I ever got. I thought Mom would pat me on the back, but boy did I get a surprise. When Mom got home, was she mad! I got one of the worst talking-tos I ever got.

There was a pond close to our shanty with big bullfrogs in it. We took a fishhook, tied it on the end of a string, and put a piece of bright-colored cloth on it. Then you let it down easy in front of a bullfrog, and gulp, you had a bullfrog.

One night I got a belly ache. I was about 12 years old. I walked the woods all night and did I have a bellyache. The next day Dr. Ross came out and checked me over. He told Mom to get me ready, and I'll take him to the hospital and take his appendix out. Well, I thought that was the end of me. But I was only in the hospital for three days and they couldn't stand me anymore, so they sent me home.

Chapter 6

Then we moved back to good old Bundysburg. It wasn't long, I started hunting coon with Hank Patchen. I used to go coon hunting with Dad before that, but Dad got his coon hounds out of the dog pound. So, you walked 50 miles for every coon you got. When you went with Hank, you got worn out carrying coon. I think Hank could have taken a Jersey heifer in the woods and treed a coon with her. Hank hunted coon enough years that he knew about how a coon would act. Old Mose was a raw-boned treeing walker and was also the best coon dog I ever hunted with. I always thought the longer a hound's ears were, the colder nose he had, or the older track he could run.

But I changed my mind with Mose. He was a medium-eared hound, and he could run a track when most dogs didn't know there was a coon around. Hank used to hunt PA and Ohio. He would always get between 100 and 200 coons in a season. PA season used to open before Ohio's so he'd go to PA for a week at a time and hunt nights and sleep days. And he'd always bring a lot of coon along home. Hank told me the fall Mose was 3 years old, he found a new place to hunt in PA. So, the first night he stopped at this bar and got to talking with some other coon hunters. They told Hank that slashing behind the bar, nobody could get any coon out of there. Swamp, grapevines, and gullies. Well, Hank told them that's where I'm going. Three hours. later he walked in there with four nice coons. Hank sat at the table and before long three other coon hunters sat at his table, eyeballing those 4 nice coons. Before it was over with, $500.00 lay on the table, cash, in front of him for old Mose, but Hank wouldn't touch it.

You, young people, don't realize how much money that was in 1952. But it was a lot of gelt.

Mose was a funny dog, a coon would mess him up about twice, and when you heard old Mose again, it was yow, yow, yow, or come an' get him. Sometimes you'd have to walk a little ways to get there, but you never had to hurry. Old Mose would tree all night. When Mose was 8 years old, he was getting like old dogs get. He was still a good dog but once in a while he'd tree and there wasn't anything there. Not very often, but too often for Hank. I also bought a still dog from Hank, and those two dogs worked together good.

Smoke, the still dog looked like a big bear. Mose was slow on the track and Smoke caught a lot of coon on the ground. You talk about something that makes your hair stand on end, when you're standing next to a cornfield with everything quiet when all at once a coon let out a squall. When Smoke caught one, he didn't squall long as he was a killer.

We caught 31 coon the first year just hunting around home. The second year we got 29 then they were pretty well thinned out. Me and my brothers had a lot of fun with those two dogs. Mose taught us a lot about coon hunting. While we had old Mose, Yam Batz, or young Dave Coblentz, kept telling me about how good a coon dog Ervin Slaubaugh had. (Huddle) So I told Dave I want to go out with this dog and see how good a dog he really is. All I heard was Buck this and Buck that, and I finally got kind of sick of it.

Well, they let me know which night they wanted to go and away we went. They had Buck and another pup and I had Smoke and old Mose. Now it wasn't a very good night as it was frosty and bright moonshine. All at once the dogs took off and didn't go far, they were treed. Very seldom Mose would run trash but that night he did. And the other dogs did, too. I had the 22 and I seen this little brown animal out on a limb. Right away I got mink in my mind and money. Up till then, I'd never seen a mink.

Well, one shot, and down he came. I stomped on him and put him in my coat pocket. That was a mistake as I ended up burning my coat. It was a weasel and what a stink. We walked a while in the bright moonshine and finally, we stopped and stood around visiting. Nothing was moving that night anyhow. Finally, about 20 feet from me Mose made a couple of tree barks on a beech tree and you could see by the moonlight, there was nothing on that tree. He kept smelling around the leaves. The other dogs went over, but the track was too old for them.

Well, everybody got a good laugh out of this, that is, everybody but me, I said, "Now, wait a minute, give old Mose a little time."

They were going to start for home. Mose monkeyed around for a while, then he sat down at that beech tree and said, yaw, yaw, yaw, or come and get him. Then they started laughing all over again. I walked around that tree and the backside was rotted out. I laid my gun down, laid on my back, and slid my head in this rotted-out spot. Took my flashlight and flashed up there and about 20 feet up there sat a nice coon.

I said, "Give me my gun." I shot up into that tree and it crawled out.

I said, "Just wait a minute and he'll come down." He did and I finished him off.

I picked him up and said, "No argument where this coon belongs, is there?" But they were headed for home.

Chapter 7

Back when I was grading kiln-dried lumber at Spartywood, one forenoon a big, chartered bus pulled in and it was full of people, Russian people. They all had something to do with sawmills, particleboard, plywood, grade lumber, etc.

Now when communism fell, these people didn't know how to do business, and that is why they came over here. The one woman and she was a nice-looking woman, was the head of a sawmill that employed 4,000 men. That's hard to believe. They were trucking logs two and three hundred miles.

They had an interpreter with them. Well, I graded lumber till dinner time, then I headed for the lunchroom. Bill Reese came in the lunchroom and informed me that I'm going down to his restaurant with him and his son Jay and Janet, and the foreign lumber salesmen for dinner. I told him; I'm not going. I had my dinner bucket open when Bill sent someone in to tell me I'm going.

So, I got up and went out in the parking lot and told Bill, "How am I going?"

Bill said get right on that bus and find a seat.

So, I did. There I sat, surrounded by Russians and the gibberish they were talking. I don't think I could ever learn their language. When we got to Bill's restaurant in Sparty, they put us in the back room. It had two long tables for people who wanted to put on private dinners or private meetings. We were sitting there, waiting on food and there were two younger men sitting across from me. One of them got out a cigarette and was going to light it and the other one gave him an elbow in the ribs. He jerked his cigarette out of his mouth and put it back in his shirt pocket. I reached in my pocket and pulled out my pipe and filled it with tobacco and lit it. He gave me a big smile and lit his cigarette. We were all nervous, but when it was all over, they are just people, the same as anywhere else. When we left the restaurant to go back to Spartywood, I asked the interpreter if any of these people could speak German. He rattled off a row of gibberish, and this little Russian came over with a smile, he was an older fellow. And he said,"Sprehen du da deutch?"

And I said, "Ya,mir sprehen alles deutch da heim." Oh, did he laugh. He just couldn't believe it. We could talk pretty good together.

Me and that man talked till they left. The woman, that was the head of the sawmill, tried talking to me, but a little English and a little Russian, I just couldn't understand. She gave me a pin of something. I don't know what it is supposed to be, but I still have it. And the man who spoke German gave me a pack of Russian postcards. I still have those, too. it was an interesting experience.

Chapter 8

One day Joe Cicatella told me he has a buddy that's in the Canadian Air Force and flies an F18 fighter jet. And he's going to buzz us tonight. I didn't say anything to the neighbors on purpose. Well, it was just dark when here he come and the neighbors shook up. He wasn't up very high. Son John was out in the barn with his gas lantern. That pilot put that jet right over son John's house and what a noise. I was out in the yard, watching him and John's gas lantern went for the house almost the speed of a car. Oh, did I laugh. The little grandkids were crying. Daughter Esther lived down the road from me and she thought it was a tornado. There was water in her basement, and she was down there, holding her kids. She didn't like the pilot. He came over our place again and headed her straight down. Son Dennis flipped his buck spotlight in his eyes, then he flipped his headlights on. This pilot had a girlfriend in Titusville and that's just 10 miles from us. He buzzed us three or four times after that and boy was that exciting. He'd flip that plane's wings straight up and down and just as quick the other way.

He did all kinds of stunts with that plane and he could handle it. Joe, down at the store, asked me if I'd like to visit with this pilot someday. I told Joe to let me know what night and we'd homemade pie and coffee. Well, Joe let me know and one night about 6:30 this pilot, and his girlfriend, and Joe drove in. We were on the porch and talked for about two hours. From the ground, it was about 20 feet to crawl up into the cockpit of that F18.

I asked him, "When you climb up that ladder, haven't you got a little fear in your heart.

He said, "None at all, "He said he has more fear walking down the road than he has in that jet.

He said when he was playing around here, he was only going about 500 miles per hr. The top speed is about 1500 mph for an F18. He said anyone who has legs too long from the hip to the knee can't be an F18 pilot. Because when they would eject it would rip their legs off on the instrument panel.

He said, "Look how big my neck is."

He had a big neck, all muscle, from bracing himself from all of those zig-zags. My son Tobe gave him a ride on his open hackey.

Joe told him, "Don't go on that thing as it sways when you go fast."

But he wanted a ride, so Tobe took him down the road about half a mile and turned around.

Tobe says, "You want to see what this horse has got?"

And he said, "Yeah."

So away they went and that hackey started swaying and he grabbed ahold and hung on.

When they got back to our place, he said," Joe, you were right, those things do sway."

Those jet pilots go through some rough training. He had one more year when he was here. He said when his time is up, the government will have papers ready to re-enlist and a check for $100,000.00. If he enlists again, the check is his, and plus he gets his paycheck once a month. I asked him what he was gonna do and he said he didn't know. Well, he didn't take it. He's flying passenger planes now. That one time he was flying around here, he set that jet on its tail and went straight up till he went through the clouds and then he was gone.

Before he here, I said, "When you come through here again, when you leave, set that jet on its tail above my house and rip her open."

He said, "It would break every window in the neighborhood."

I said, "I changed my mind. Bring it down low and put it right over our house and bring it down where we can see you." About two weeks later he did it and we saw him.

Chapter 9

Now, back in my younger years, I obeyed the game laws pretty close except when I got the dates mixed up when coon season started and little things like that. But after I moved to Spartansburg, some of my hunting buddies got me to ease up a little bit. I think what started me off was when the little wife was ahead on woodchucks. she should have known better. Its hard to beat an old 30-30 and sometimes when I'd get behind and got desperate, well, what are you gonna do. I would always try to keep a straight face when one of my buddies would miss a chuck. I guess they tried, too. But you could usually see that little smirk on their face. The same smirk Mattie used to have when she was ahead. Boy, I used to like to go out after work and wipe that smirk off her face by getting 2 or 3 chucks. One night, me and Joe were hunting chucks and I was behind, of course. We were on this little dirt road and we came up to a sharp curve, and whoa, there sat a nice chuck.

Joe said, "If you open the door, he'll duck."

Well, there was just one thing to do, and that was stick the gun out the window and shoot. And that's what Joe told me to do.

He said, "I'll watch traffic! So, I did, and Boom, a dead chuck. I straightened up in the seat and there set a pickup, nose to nose with Joe's pickup. Well, I was lucky, it was a friend of ours.

Then Joe had the nerve to holler at the guy and say, "If he ever does that again, he'll never go hunting with me again."

One night me and Joe, and Tony Rose, another good hunting buddy, were going chuck hunting. We were having a hard thunderstorm when Joe and Tony pulled in. Son Dennis and family were at our place that and Dennis is afraid of storms. Joe Tony pulled right up to the entrance door. Dennis was standing there, holding the door open, and was watching the storm. Well, one of these guys flipped an M80 right in front of the door and Dennis didn't see it. When it went off, Dennis about came apart. He thought that was the end of him. I laughed so hard, I didn't even care if I didn't get any chucks.

Tony Rose is a serious hunter, and he didn't miss very often. But I remember one time when he did miss. It was contest night, and me and Tony were hunting together. We were way off the road, next to a field.

I said, "Tony, there is one on your side."

Tony stopped the truck and laid his gun out the window and Boom. This chuck was right on the edge of the weeds, and when Tony shot, he went in the weeds. I seen Tony stomping around, so I went down to see. Tony didn't pick up a woodchuck. We found a little blood trail down to the chuck's hole and that's when Tony started his Indian war dance and was talking some of their Indian war language.

I had to turn my back so he wouldn't see me smile. I didn't want to smile, but I couldn't help it.

Tony Rose has a brother living in Montana. John is a good friend of mine. He also has a son Mike living out there. He is also a good friend of mine. John is in his early 90's and he walks better than I do. Old John was a hunting guide for years, now his son John and Tony's son Mike are hunting guides.

I met young John a couple of times and him and Tony's son Mike are hard as nails. Out of all my hunting buddies, I'm the only one who hunts with a 30-50 so you can imagine all the flak I have to take. But they have to admit, I have a 30-30 that will shoot. Some of my buddies say all a 30-30 is good for is a stove poker or a jack handle.

Now, son Noah bought himself a 25-06, and you ought to hear him brag. Last year I shot a deer, over 300 yards, running. I tried to tell him it was just a lucky shot, but I can't tell my boys anything. They must get their bullheadedness from their mother as I never thought I was like that.

These seven boys and five girls were raised on deer and I taught them everything about deer hunting that I know, but now I don't know anything. The thing they don't understand is deer hunting is partly skill and part luck. My luck has always run right along with Pat McManus, that writes in the Outdoor Life. I think Pat, like me, is a good enough hunter but he just hasn't got the luck that some hunters have.

But I've shot my share of deer, even if some of my buddies don't think so. When Noah was 16 or 17, he knew it all, but he was having trouble hitting a deer. I told him, hold that gun down. So, what does he do? He started shooting them through the both feet. I think it was the same day I walked out back after dinner, it was doe season, and Huh? there laid a deer. I up and shot boom, and that thing took off like a jet airplane. I boomed her again and down she went. I thought to myself, now why was that deer laying there. I started looking her over, and she was shot through both front feet. The first thing that popped into my mind was, Noah. See what I mean. I tried, anyhow.

But anyway, let them buy and hunt with what they want, it's their money. I'll stick with my old 30-30. Maybe this fall, I can go deer hunting again, if I keep gaining. I missed the last four years. I'd sure like to see another one fall.

When I lived in back of me on the farm,(this was after I keeled over while hunting, with a brain aneurism, that one fall I didn't feel good.) I told Mom, I'm going out in my workshop the first day of buck season and if I see anything, alright, and if I don't, it's alright, too. My workshop was right on the edge of the woods. Mom didn't like me hunting by myself since I keeled over years ago, and I don't like to hunt with the boys. I've shot several deer when the boys were with me but they make me nervous. And then they make up those big tales about how I act and breathe when I see a deer. Well, the first morning I got ready. Mom said she wants to make a pot of chili, then she would come out and help me watch for deer. I went out and fired up the furnace and it was starting to get warmed up Now I knew my boys were laughing behind my back. But one thing they forgot was, I hunted on this place a few more years than they did.

It wasn't over 15 minutes I was watching out the window and, "Hey! There's a deer!"

I looked and it was a buck. Slowly, I opened the window, blood pressure going up fast. Boom! Down he went.

Now, when the boys wanted to hear my deer story, right here is where it should have stopped. But anyway, it didn't. I told them just how it went. I shot and down he went. I watched and he started thrashing around and boom, I gave him another one. Having a little trouble holding the gun still. I watched a little more and he started thrashing again and boom, I gave him another one, the gun didn't want to hold still at all. I watched and that time he laid still. So, I went down to look my trophy over. Now here is where the luck part comes in. It was a 4-point, but it could just as well have been a 12-point if I would have had a little luck.

Well, about this time Mom started hollering and I said, "Hey, I'm right here. Come and look what I got."

It was just a 4-point, but a nice 4-point, if you know what I mean. Well, that night the boys skinned him out and got him ready for the table. I had a little smirk on my face, as that was the only deer for the cider family that day. Now when the boys skinned this buck, they couldn't find a bullet hole.

Now here's the luck factor again. Why couldn't they just skin the buck and let it go at that? No, they had to get nosey, but they couldn't find that bullet hole. So, they got the head and started skinning it and there was a bullet hole, but only one. Maybe all the bullets went in the same hole.

Every once in a while, Joe Cicatella will say, "Cider, how many bucks have you shot in your lifetime?"

I'll say, "Joe, I've never counted them."

Then he'll laugh. Truth is, I have shot quite a few of both, and I've never had horn soup. Don't think I'd care for it at all. We raised 12 children and we just weren't that fussy. Deer meat was better than no meat.

Our oldest son, Ervin, you could depend on him to make a mistake in the first day or two. I'd usually chew him out, but in a nice, friendly way. Son Billy, that one year, shot 30 sometimes and all he had was a piece of bone, about 2 inches long. The next year he wanted to borrow my 30- 30 in doe season.

I said, "Don't spoil that gun that's a one-shot gun."

Billy brought the gun home the first night and I said, "How many shots?"

Billy said, "One "

And I said, "Atta boy."

I had the trigger pull lightened and put a weaver K4 wideview-scope on it and that's when me and that little 30-30 started having fun. My boys will admit one thing, in deer season, when Dad's gun cracked, there was usually meat for the table 90% of the time. I might have stretched that just a little bit. That buck I shot from my workshop. Al Cox, the auctioneer said that buck had hoof rot from standing on a pile of apples covering a salt block. Another one of my so-called buddies. Oh, well, you just laugh right with them and just keep on eating deer meat.

Chapter 10

Folks, I get days I feel pretty bad, then I have good days, too. Last week I had some company that really picked me up. One night Eli Hostetler and wife and Herby Gibbs and wife walked in the door. Now me and Herby go back a long way. He was the first man to beat me in a foot race for years. But I can outrun him now. Herby lost one leg to sugar diabetes.

Herby set here and said, "You make me feel good."

I said, "Why?"

"I can see you are in worse shape than I am," he said.

Huh! I was thinking the same thing when I looked at Herby. I thought he was in worse shape than I am. We both lost all our excess fat but hopefully, we can gain a little of it back.

Then one-night Jitter and wife, and his son-in-law Mikie Shnikie and Ed Troyer and wife and Marty and Edward were here. They are two of Ed's special children and believe me, they are special to me.

Then one afternoon this little car pulled in and this tall guy got out and I knew him right away. Kenny Tillery and wife Carol. My brother Andy and wife Ida were along. Big Kenny lifted Andy out of the car and put him in his wheelchair. It hurts me to see my brother in that kind of shape. At least I've still got him. Well, it's just this simple, the Cider boys that worked the hardest are wearing out first. Brother Bim isn't showing any wear and tear yet. I told Bim I'm writing another book and he said, "Well, keep the lies out of it!"

Chapter 11

My mind goes back to 36 years ago when we move time to Sparty. Before we moved, we bought groceries in Quinn's Market in Bloomfield, Ohio. A lot of the time I bought the groceries, so I still remember some of the prices. I think taxis were 10¢ a mile. Hamburg, wieners, bologna, and bacon were 3 lbs. for a dollar. Salad dressing was 59¢ a qt. Ice cream cones were 5¢,10¢, and 15¢ for three scoops. Sounds good, doesn't it?

But we didn't make much money in those days. Now if my boys don't make 6 or 7 hundred dollars a week, they're hurting. But the way hospital bills went up, I feel sorry for young people. Everything is high anymore. Cost of living, taxes, hospitals and you name it. A $100.00 dollar bill today is like a $20.00 bill was back then. I remember when lucky strike cigarettes were 17¢ a pack, and camels were 21¢. Now, look what they cost. Oh, well I don't have to worry about that anymore. I could hardly afford Prince Albert anymore. Now when our 12 kids were all at home and you put three lbs. of wieners on the table, you'd better get your fork in there or you'd haul back empty.

That reminds me of another auctioneer I knew years ago. Old Tennessee Andy. A lot of you people reading this book remember old Andy. He told the people one night when I came up here from Tennessee, I had patent leather shoes on my feet, leather all around, feet pattin on the ground.

Another night he said, "you folks might wonder why I'm so little and scrawny. was raised poor."

They lived in a little house. It wasn't a big house but it was home. There were enough pork chops for each of the kids and one for Mom and Dad. He said he doesn't know where his Dad got the pork chops, as hard up as they were. There was one pork chop left on the plate and Andy and all his brothers and sisters wanted that pork chop. It was summertime and they had a screen door and an oil lamp. Andy said a puff of wind came in the screen door and almost blew out the lamp, but it lit up again. He said when it lit up, he had the pork chop but had three forks sticking in his hand.

Andy used to have an auction in Mespo years ago. He used to sell a lot of suitcases. I think he got them at airports, train stations, and bus depots. Probably suitcases that people had left there. It was a little like gambling because nobody knew what was in them, then he'd auction them off. We got clothes, money, jewel watches, and army socks you could hardly wear out. Oh, those were the good old days.

You could go to town with $20.00 and come home with a whole buggy load of groceries. I remember when we were first married, we spent $12.00 a week for groceries. Now if we go out for supper, which isn't very often, usually it's $14-$15 dollars. I always have to think back, that used to buy a week's groceries. The cost of living went way up in my short lifetime of 63 yrs. But what went up the fastest was doctors and hospitals. When my youngest daughter was born in Union City Hospital, the next day my wife had major surgery, was in surgery for one hour and 40 minutes mother and baby were in the hospital for 7 days. What would that cost today? My hospital bill was a few dollars over $600.00. But at that time, I think I was getting $3.50 per hr. So, your paycheck wasn't very big. A poor man today doesn't have a chance. Just hope you don't get sick. There are a lot of doctors out there who still have a heart. Dr. Nazzarro was one of them. Dr. Henderson was another one. Radiation Dr. in Franklin Hospital Dr. Dragon and Dr. Pirogos are two more and there have been other ones, too.

Chapter 12

Now my mind goes back to good old Bundysburg and those big old steam engines. I've always wished my boys could stand on that bank when those steam engines went up through there with 100 cars of coal. It was uphill and they were wrapped around three curves and those engines had to work. And noise with a capital "N". A lot of times they'd throw off candy and beings as I was the oldest, I was the one that got it most of the time. One time a train came down the hill empty and going a pretty good clip. The engineer leaned out the window with a bag of candy in his hand. Us four boys were standing there waiting. He threw it and my hands were up waiting, and that candy went between my hands and hit me right between the eyes and I hit the deck, kerbang. I bounced up just like a rubber ball, but the boys had the candy and were long gone. It was a bag of hard butterscotch candy.

One day a train came down the hill, just going slow. The engine stopped right on the crossing. Of course, us boys were right there. The engineer crawled off the engine with a fair-sized box. Of course, us four boys were right there with stretched hands, but he said", Oh no, this time the girls get the candy." We took a disliking to that man right then and there. And my three little sisters were loaded with candy. And Mother didn't make them share with us, either. Oh well, we grew up anyway.

Chapter 13

I was up to Roswell Cancer Institute again and had another cat scan and they say these three spots on my right lung have grown a little bit. They wanted me to go on chemo right away but I said I'm not interested. I've heard too much about that stuff. They checked my liver with the cat scan and say that's O.K. I had lots of doctors talked to me and I finally said I'd consider surgery.

They said lung surgery is a hard surgery and it would be too quick after my other surgery when they almost cut my head off. Wasn't quite that bad, but it was bad. They also want to wait and see if any more spots show up. I told them I can hardly believe it as I feel good for the shape I'm in. I'm eating better, gaining weight, and getting stronger every day. But they say this is just starting. They also wanted to do a biopsy, but I said no. When they took a biopsy of my throat last winter, that fired things up pretty good.

I have friends in Townville, PA Leonard and Mary Zook. Mary had cancer for, I would say, 12 or 14 years. She sent some herbs and vitamins over and I started taking them today. My next appointment is November 24 but it will probably be in December. Because they have a new cancer pill out for my kind of cancer and I said I would do that, just one pill a day. The prescription he gave me, he said don't take it to a drug store, it would cost you $6,000.00. That's six thousand dollars. They want me to take it for 8 weeks before they do another cat scan. They told us what to do and they'd probably give us the pills. I know I'm not going to buy them for $50.00 a pill. I don't have much faith in them as they said it only helps 15 or 20% of the people who take them. So we'll just wait and see.

Chapter 14

The good old days of the Slab and Grab lumber were the good old days but I didn't know it. Some of my flippen boys, you didn't know what they were gonna do next and I still don't. The first years the Slab and Grab ran, I sawed myself. I wasn't old, but close to 40, and about 2:30 I'd get pretty tired. One night I snuck up to Centerville to a beer distributor and got me a case of Old German beer. Right across the road from the mill, there were about four acres of timber, grapevine, and brush. I took that case of beer over and hid it real good in a brush pile.

About 2:30 I'd get pretty tired then we'd take a break and I'd sneak over and drink a cold beer. That would really pick me up. Well, this one day it was really warm, and I could hardly wait for 2:30 to come. Finally, it was 2:30 and we shut down. sauntered over to the woods unconcerned but when I got to the brush, I speeded up. I got over to the brush patch and everything was gone. There were probably a dozen bottles left and you would have thought they'd leave me one bottle. It must have been coon or squirrels as it wasn't any of my boys. I'll say one thing for those boys, they sure could keep a straight face.

Now we sawed for Spartywood and they gave us an old Petibone that looked like it went through two wars and a fire, but it ran. Well, anyway, when I'd get low on diesel fuel, I'd drive it to Buell's Store and fill it up and put it on Spartywood's bill. It had a 353 GM Gutless miracle under the hood. Then I'd get a cup of coffee before heading back to the sawmill.

That's when Joe Cicatella would have his fun. That one time me and Dana Martin were having coffee and Dana said, "There's a State cop up there talking to Joe and they keep looking back here."

Lucky, I didn't have the high lift that night. I told Dana I'd better go up there and see what Joe is stirring up.

I walked up to them and heard Joe tell him, "Yeah, that's all he does is drive that high lift up and down the road, no license plates on it, and he doesn't have a driver's license."

I felt better when I looked at the cop because I knew him.

I said, "I'm going to tell you like it is. I saw for Spartywood and it is their high lift and I'm not going to buy their fuel. So, when I run low, I drive down here and fill it up."

"It isn't even a half-mile. I am not breaking the law.", I said.

He said, "Technically, you're breaking the law."

I said, "Yeah, a little bit."

Joe said, "Can I make a citizen's arrest?"

The cop said, "Sure you can."

Joe said, "How do; write him up?"

The cop said, "You arrest him and call me and I'll write him up."

I said, "You guys don't worry me." (Inside I was shaking in my shoes, but they didn't know it)

I said, "You have to catch me in the act."

The cop said, "Cider Dan, if I caught you on the road with that thing, you could probably talk your way out of it."

I said, "Yeah, I think I could."

But he said, "If one of these rookie cops would catch you, they would probably slap handcuffs on you."

Boy, that made Joe laugh. He said he'd like to have a picture of that. One day I was grading lumber somewhere and the boys were running the mill shorthanded when the lift ran low on fuel. When I came home that night, between Buell's and the mill was a swamp, there were two evenly spaced ditches through that swamp. Well, one of the boys took the lift to Buell's, probably flying low as that thing would really move in high gear, and lost control, and down in the swamp he went. But you know something, it wasn't his fault. That was one nice thing about my boys, it didn't much matter what they did, it wasn't their fault.

Anyway, they had to get a log truck to get pulled out. It just didn't go so good when Dad left the mill. When the cat's away, the mice will play. One day it was real icy. I couldn't back out after putting logs on the skidway and I was rocking back and forth and that 353 Detroit was really bellering when all at once, Ker wham! I thought the Russians dropped a bomb and made a direct hit. I looked and there stood Dana Martin with a slab in his hand and a grin on his face. I had some thoughts that weren't very nice. He was trying to get my attention and he finally got it. That cab was steel and when he hit that, what a bang that was.

Our son Andy was our wonder boy. We'd wonder what he'd do next. And we still do. The other night this one-horse wagon went past, going a pretty good clip.

Mom hollered out and said, "Did you see who was driving that horse?"

I said, "No."

And she said, "Two of Whitey's little boys."

They are only 8 and 9 years old and I thought, knowing Whitey, who knows. I took off for son Dennis, down the road a hop, skip, and a jump

I asked Dennis, "Did you see who was driving that one horse wagon that went past."

He said, "Whitey."

I said, "He wasn't driving when he went past our place."

He laid down in the wagon box when he went past here, then got up and sat on his seat again after he was passed. Is it any wonder why my hair and whiskers are snow white? I was never a guy for much horseplay, they must get it from their mother.

I'll have to put this in this book. when we lived back in the big house, I got a gorilla mask somewhere. It was an awful-looking thing. Well, I had a lot of fun with that thing, scaring the grandkids, and other kids, too.

I had a little room in the big house. I had my rolltop desk in there and my guns, etc. I also had an office chair by the desk. Always had dark curtains on the windows. One day I went in there to get something, I was in a hurry when all at once I went SCREEEEECHEH I let out a scream worse than any woman you ever heard. There in my chair sat a little black man. Mom and Clara(my other wonder child) took that mask and they took clothes and made a little man out of it. They put one my old floppy hats on him and a black coat with floppy sleeves and there he sat. That was one of the worst scares I ever had.

Son Dennis works over at Brush Run Lumber Saws on an automatic sawmill. A couple of weeks ago they bought a piece of timber up in Erie. Well, Dennis cut the logs. The first Monday he threw a tree on a pickup truck. The next week he smashed his power saw. The next Monday morning, when he walked into Brush Run's lunchroom, Cripple Billy said, "Well, Dennis, the first-week cutting logs you smashed a pickup. The next week you smashed a power saw, so what have you got in mind to smash this week?"

Dennis said, "Your mouth if you don't shut it."

That doesn't sound very nice, but Dennis and Billy are good friends.

When the kids were all at home, it seemed I was always one jump behind. One night at Halloween, they snuck out and went Halloweening. I don't know where all but they were at Joe Slaubaugh's. They took hay out of the barn and lit it in the driveway. Well, Joe saw this and he didn't know what was coming off so he went and called the cops. Well by then they were standing in a fairly long driveway. They saw this car coming down the blacktop and he was flying low.

They said, "That's no cop, he's going too fast."

Well, all at once that car hit the brakes and wheeled in the driveway and there he had them all in his car lights. Our youngest daughter was only 15 and she ran and laid in the ditch. He didn't get her Now the cop started asking questions. He knew Whitey and for a good reason.

He said, "Whitey, where do you work? "

And Whitey said, "After tonight, probably nowhere."

The cop said, "Joe Slaubaugh."

They just got a warning, and I didn't even know they were gone. Brad Allen, the cop was a good friend of mine. We came home from town one day with a taxi and a state cop followed us in. The driver got all shook up.

I said, "Cool down, that's my buddy", and it was Brad.

We set in the yard and visited till he got a call about some 4-wheelers tearing up and down the road.

One fall, a man stopped in and wanted us to keep 8 ponies here for the winter. They were from a place that kept troubled children. They made it sound real good, they would furnish hay and feed and still pay us. I only seen him once that winter, I fed my hay until spring. And one day he drove in. He paid me for everything. My kids are all grown up now, but they still talk about how much fun they had with those ponies.

We lived in a basement house that winter and couldn't see out towards the road. And it's a good thing. These ponies weren't shod and those kids would go down the road about a quarter-mile to the dip in the road, and turn around and race back. I still don't know why nobody got hurt.

Chapter 15

It was about this time that John Byler moved out here. He was just like a colt that was tied up all winter, then all at once turned loose. This was easy money John that hails from Clintonville. I used to work with John on a sawmill and I'm still trying to forget those days, but I can't quite do it. I bet Levi Byler can't forget them either. Really, those were the good old days, but we just didn't know it.

What that boy didn't think of, wasn't to be thought of. I remember one time at Halloween, John and some of his buddies stopped in that night, we gave them cookies and coffee and visited awhile. I thought, boy we'll escape this year. I went out with them to help them hitch up and make sure they got out of here. Got up the next morn. and looked out, there was my buggy upside down, four wheels sticking straight up. Went Out to the barn and some of the jerseys were harnessed up, and oh, what a mess.

Some of John's buddies were Chubby's John and Ben, Mahlon's Ben and Eli, and some more I can't think of. Now them boys could really cut a shine. I think if I would have had four boys in a row like that, I think I would have put my head down and run into a cement wall. But anyhow, we survived.

We came home from church one Sunday and there were two calves tied to the footboard of our bed, chickens were on the table, cackling and dropping from behind. The rooster was on the table, crowing, cats and you name it was in the house. My little wife was one mad woman. Didn't do her much good to go to church that day.

Well, anyhow, John got married. He contracted to run Dick Nichol's sawmill. I didn't work there, but I heard all kinds of things that went on there. There was an old outhouse, the outback that everybody used, as there was no bathroom. One day Mel Gingerich was sitting in there and John got some gas and poured it outside and it ran inside on the floor. It was a rickety old thing. Well, anyway, he lit it. I heard it first, Mel came out of there with his pants down, but I guess he had them up.

Another time somebody, don't remember who, was sitting in there, and here comes John with the high lift and got one fork under it and flipped it on the side. I bet whoever was in there won't forget that ride. Sometimes John comes out on the wrong end. This last deer season, John had a pretty good shanty. The first day he didn't see a deer.

He made a remark to his son Paul, and his son-in-law, he said, "I ought to burn it down."

So, a day or two later they went past John's shanty and John wasn't in it so they lit it and burned it down. A few days later when John went hunting, all he had left was a pile of ashes. John, it's called hunting season, not setting season.

Another time John came out on the wrong end, he was just a boy, probably 9 or 10 years old his mother and dad were visiting their daughters, the Andy Millers. Now John's nephew Bob and John were about the same age. Bob had to go to the outhouse. There was a knothole in the side of the outhouse and John couldn't behave. John got a stick and poked it in the hole. Bob grabbed it and pulled it out of his hand. Then he stuck the end down the hole into you know what then stuck it out the hole again and John grabbed it again, and what a surprise! John, in my first book I left you pretty well alone, so stay tuned.

Chapter 16

A couple of weeks ago Amelia Byler from Mercer Co, widow of Jake Byler, and Harvey Byler's Marie were here awhile in the afternoon. Amelia has had cancer for 16 years. She is 72 years old and still gets around by herself. She is a swell person. A couple days ago one of my old Bundysburg buddies stopped in for a visit. Mike John's Eli and wife.

Brings to mind something that happened when I was about 15 years old. Eli still recalled it. Old Elmer Yoder's had church and it was warm. After church' I saw Eli head for the milk house to get a drink of water. I don't remember where I got the half pail of water. Eli was getting a drink when I poured the water all over him and then I took off for the woods and said, "Feet, do your thing?

Well, here came Eli with a pail and some water. He didn't go very far; he saw he had a problem. He stopped and yanked his shoes off and then the race was on. We went cross lots and did we go. Finally, we could hardly go anymore. We came to the B&0 railroad.

There was a woven wire fence along the railroad. I got over the fence and fell. I could not get up anymore. Eli fell over the fence on top of me. He got a little water on me. Then we lay there and panted like a couple of dogs. After we got our breath back, we had to walk back. Those were the good old days' and we didn't even know it.

Eli looks a lot younger than his years and I look a lot older. Like I was run over with a Mack truck. I never took very good care of myself, but with 12 children, the last thing on your mind is taking care of yourself.

Brings to mind something else, son Noah did while we were trying to farm as a hobby. One day he came in the milk house with a big hand full of horse manure.

He told one of the boys, "Take the cover off the milk can."

The boys said, "What are you going to do?"

Noah said, "Listen, the old man doesn't know it, but he's going to go under, farming, and if we can get him shut off from the milk company, he'll sell the cows."

He put that big hand full of manure in that can of milk. And you know what, I didn't even get a tag out of it. The guy dumping milk that day must have been out the night before or had a bottle of hootch in his pocket. The milk company was Carnation. $4.12 per hundred for 3.5 milk. Old Pudge, one of my so-called friends hinted I had six and two cows; 6 quarts of grain and two quarts of milk. But those were the good old days, we just didn't know it.

Chapter 17

Now my thoughts go back to old Sparty- wood. Our foreman was Buzzy Vanderhoff. Well, Buzzy wasn't my foreman but he thought he was so we just left it at that. I should have worded that a little different. Buzzy was my when it suited me.

Well, anyway, what I wanted to tell everybody, I wasn't that bad a guy when I started working for Spartywood, but little by little Buzzy got me on his track. One morning I was in the lunchroom at 6:30 in the morning. Buzzy motioned me into the big office. He never said a word, just picked up the telephone and called my brother Bim up in Middlefield, OH. Now that's hard to believe that a foreman, this time of the morning, could think of something like that. Bim answered the phone.

Buzzy said, "Is this Eli J. Byler?"

And Bim said, "Yes."

Buzzy said, "I'm from the Internal Revenue Service and we have a little problem with your tax return for the last two years!"

Meanwhile Buzzy pushed a button on the telephone and I could hear everything that Bim said.

Bim said, "What's the problem?"

Buzzy said, "there are several problems." Boy, I heard Bim was one nervous boy. Buzzy said, "I think I'd better come out and so over your books, will you be at home tomorrow?"

Bim said, "I'll be hanging around the barn somewhere." (He told me later he meant by the neck.)

Well, by this time I couldn't hold it any longer and I started laughing. He knew he'd been had and was he mad. So Buzzy told him it's his brother Dan and this was all his idea. I didn't even know what Buzzy was gonna do. I tried to tell Bim that Buzzy was lying but Buzzy was so convincing, Bim believed him Buzzy could sell ice to an Eskimo. So that's how my day started that day.

Joe Cicatella, at the Buell's Store heard about this and he had to have his fun. That night he called Bim from the Buell's Store to see if he'd rat on his brother.

He got him on the phone and said, "This is Corporal Dean from the Corry, PA Police Barracks." He said he received a call stating that you got a telephone call from somebody impersonating an I R S officer and that is a felony, prison time. Is this true?"

Bim said, "Yes, it's true."

Joe said, "Have you got any idea who this man was?"

Bim said, "All he knows is the guy's name is Buzzy and he's foreman at Spartywood."

Now Joe wanted to see if he'd rat on his own brother, so he said, "My report said there was another man with him, do you have any idea who it was?"

Bim says, "Yeah, it was my Dan J. Byler from Spartansburg, PA WHAM! Bim was still mad. Well, then Joe started laughing and told Bim who he was. When Bim hung up the phone, he told his wife Alta, if I get one more phone call today, I am going to rip this phone right out of the wall. When I'd get in trouble at Spartywood for horseplay, Buzzy was usually involved. One time he wasn't involved. He was mad at Peter Rabbit that one morning and threatened to shoot him. He didn't mean it, but you know when a man makes a statement like that, it kinda gets you thinking. By this time Joe Cicatella, Buzzy, and some of the other guys had me pretty well ruined when it comes to horseplay.

Right away my mind started turning, you know what I mean. I had to get some mileage out of this. Now, I don't remember who all was involved, but Buzzy wasn't one of them. Peter was laying stickers in the stacker building. They'd open the big doors and take out the empty boxes and set in a full one. Well, the forks of the high lift usually had a little gravel on them and when they'd moved the boxes around some would always drop off. I just thought to myself, if someone would sneak outside and throw an M80 under the sticker box, the gravel would fly. There were about 8 inches between the floor and the bottom of the sticker box. Well, I don't remember who had the M80 on who threw it, but it worked perfect. Boom and that gravel must have hit him in the legs. The sticker box was almost empty and Peter dove into the sticker box headfirst. When he knew this was a joke, he was one mad guy.

You know, that's the trouble with a lot of people, especially women, they have no sense of humor. Me and Buzzy are still good friends, but I miss those days.

I have another good friend who used to work at Spartywood. He is one nice guy and we've always been good friends. I'm not going to put his name in here because we are still good friends and I want to keep it that way.

Like all young fellows, he'd get in trouble once in a while. One day, one of Don Patterson's pilers got called in the conference room. He opened the door, and two cops were waiting on him, slapped the cuffs on him, and away they went. Right away this guy says if you get called into the conference room, it's time to head for the woods. Well, right away something clicked in my brain. See what Buzzy and Joe did to me.) Break time that day I told Buzzy and Buzzy said he'll take care of it. I put Don wise and the next afternoon someone came out and hollered (I'll name him Geno, not his real name)

He said," Geno, you are wanted in the conference room."

Of course, we were all watching. Geno looked back towards the woods and went on piling lumber.

Don said, "Geno, you'd better go."

Pretty soon the guy came out and said, "Geno, they want you in the conference room right now."

Geno looked towards the woods but finally he went, he walked real slow, his shoulders hunched as though, "I've had it." He walked up to the conference room door and knocked.

Buzzy said, "Come in."

Geno stepped inside and there sat Buzzy laughing. Boy, he didn't have much of a sense of humor that day as he was one mad guy. Well, he came out to the grading shed and went past where I was grading lumber.

He stopped and pointed his finger at me and said "YOU!" real loud.

He didn't even look at me for two days.

The third day at noon he came up and sat beside me and said, "Cider, I can't stay mad at you."

And I said, "I don't want you to."

I said it's just something that had to be done. So, another day at Spartywood.

Another time, it was in the summertime and everyone was in that big lunchroom, eating dinner. Now Peter Rabbit(John Host.) was a jumpy guy. Now when Peter got ahold of a newspaper, he was in another world, so it seemed. He would concentrate on what he'd read.

This day he sat at one of the long tables on a bench with somebody's newspaper, elbows on the table, sleeves rolled up, reading the newspaper. Somebody came in the side door, I don't remember who it was, but he had a live garter snake about two feet long. He laid this snake next to Rabbit's bare arm, but he didn't notice. I was watching as I don't like snakes. This snake started crawling across Rabbit's bare arm, but it didn't register right away. All at once, Peter looked and there he was face to face with this snake. Well, I wanna tell you, things started happening and fast. Rabbit was over 6 foot tall with long arms and legs and all parts were working right then. He jumped up, the bench flew and that big table almost tipped over, and out the door he went, just hitting the high spots. That was one deal I had nothing to do with. But even now, when I sit and think of it, I have to laugh.

Jeff and Scotty Kemp, my sticker men knew I was afraid of mice. Scotty was 16 years old and full of it. But anyway we taught him a few tricks. The liftman would set in two big packs of dry kilned lumber and shove them together. I'd crawl up on top and work my way down to the ground. Well, they were big packs and you stand up on top, you was in the air. It was summer and after dinner, I crawled up on two new packs of lumber and stood up and all at once there was a mouse right in front of my face. Well, I played airplane right now. I made kind of a rough landing. Well, here those guys got a dead mouse and when I was in the lunchroom, they took dark string and tied it to the mouse and put it over the light right above my head and tied the string over in the corner. When I got on the pile of lumber, they loosened the string and let the mouse down. I didn't win them all.

Another time at Spartywood, big Jeff, and I don't remember who else were my pilers at the time. Scotty Kemp was Don's Stickerman. He worked right across the green chain from us. Scotty chewed snuff and always left his can lying next to where he worked. One day we were waiting on lumber and Scotty had gone into the lunchroom. Well, these guys got Scotty's snuff can and took it and found a couple of worms and chopped them in little pieces and mixed it in his snuff. They told me what they done. I thought Scotty would it. We got lumber again and here comes Scotty. We kept working, but we were all watching. He piled stickers awhile, grabbed his snuff box, and took a big chew.

They let him chew awhile, then they went over and asked him, "Is your snuff good today?"

He said, "Yeah."

They said, "You know you are chewing worms."

He didn't believe it, so they showed it to him and boy, was he spitting out snuff. I don't know if Scotty still chews or not, but he didn't for a long while.

I didn't have anything to do with that, but it just seemed that when something happened at Spartywood all eyes would be on me. There were about 50 or 60 other Amish guys that worked there, but I always got the blame Once in a while, I was mixed up in the soup.

One time Buzzy had a dentist appointment. He had to take antibiotics for three or four days before his appointment. Then he didn't come to work. He claimed the pills were making him sick. What was making him sick was fear; FEAR plain and simple. Well, my wife and girls knew Dr. Long, the dentist from Titusville. I didn't know him myself. I told mom what I would like to do and she said, go ahead, Dr. Long would go for that. So the next day was Buzzy's appointment. I called Dr. Long's office that forenoon and his wife answered. She was his secretary.

I said, "This is Cider Dan."

She said, "Hi, when are you going to come down and get acquainted?"

I said, "We're going to get acquainted right now. You have a Leon Vanderhoff, Jr. that has an appointment to get a tooth pulled, right?"

She said, "Yes, we have."

I said, "He's my foreman and that man is scared. Would Dr. Long go along with a little prank?"

She said, "Oh, yes."

I said, "Allright, here's what I want him to do. Look in Buzzy's mouth and tell him he has to use the big needle to numb it. Tell him he has to run it up almost to his eyes."

Well, Dr. Long did just as I told him. Buzzy got pale. Dr. Long went out the door and came in with a horse needle he had to scare people.

Buzzy saw that needle and he put up his hands and said, "Whoa, Whoa, Whoa!"

And then he got real pale. Dr. Long said he almost had him on the floor. He had to let smoke a cigarette before he pulled his tooth.

Dr. Long told him, "This wasn't my idea. An Amish man called me from Spartywood this forenoon and told me what to do. But I'm not going to tell you who it was."

Buzzy said, "You don't have to."

See what I mean. Well, about 3:30 Buzzy walked into the grading shed, madder than a wounded bear, mouth full of cotton, fists in the air. He crawled on my lumber pile and I thought he was gonna knock me off that lumber pile. Fear and common sense kept him from it. HE. HE.

Well, anyway, the shoe was on the other foot and Buzzy didn't like it. Now here's what I meant, of all the other Amish guys working at Spartywood, he picked me. No questions asked. Well, it just happened that time he was right. And another day at Spartywood.

Another time at Spartywood, we were working away, then we ran out of lumber. Jeff and the other piler went outdoors and they found this little snake. It was dead. It was about 5" long and about as big around as a pencil. Well, in the door they came and across Don's chain. Scotty looked up from Piling stickers and away he went. He was afraid of snakes. His left his glove laying there so Jeff picked one glove up and held it open and put that little snake in Scotty's glove.

Well, we got lumber and went back to work, but we kept watching for Scotty. Here he come and he was buried in stickers. He started grabbing them by the armful and piling them. Then he got a sliver in his hand. He stopped to pull the sliver out of his hand and grabbed his gloves and put them on. Now that was a new kind of dance if that's what it was; feet a-stamping, arms a-flailing and he finally got under motion, and could that guy move. Now I don't want people to think that's all we did at Spartywood because we did work, too.

Chapter 18

Now my mind goes back to Chalker Lumber Co. and when us four boys worked for Leon Chalker. We ran his sawmill, we ran his sugar bushes, put up hay and you name it. Chalker had two airplanes, but that story will remain untold. Anyway, we made a little money and everybody ate better.

I almost got killed one day pulling a lumber truck with a Ford tractor. The tractor had snap tracks on the hind wheels. When the wheels would spin, they would open up like cleats on a bulldozer web. Leon had a load of lumber on the truck and it was muddy and rainy and he got stuck. I hooked on the truck with the tractor, feet all muddy, and put pressure on the log chain I kept raising the hydraulics a little at a time and all at once the tractor reared. I stomped on the clutch and it came down part ways and my foot slipped off the clutch. She reared again and I mean quick. I stomped on the clutch again and it came down part ways and my foot slipped off again and that time it reared almost straight up. I knew I had to keep my foot on the clutch and that time I did. Those front wheels hit the ground with a crash. I sat in the rain a while just glad I was still alive. Then I pulled that truck out very carefully.

Leon's dad could build about anything. He took the rear end of a Model T and built a two-wheeled trailer. The transmission was on the front of the tongue. Now you hook a ford tractor on the trailer and he had a shaft that telescoped and you hooked that on the power take-off of the tractor. Then you'd put the transmission in low gear and the tractor in third gear and put your power take-off in gear and you had a four-wheel drive. The tractor had those old-fashioned knobby tires on it. When sugaring time came, we'd put an 8-barrel tank on the trailer to gather sap. You couldn't get that rig stuck and believe me, we tried. It would go through swamps and you name it. The other tractor had an old cab on it and a 6-barrel tank on the hydraulic bars on the back.

Now Leon's dad would put foot pedals on the tractors and then there was no governor. They would go about 35 mph and that was flying low for a tractor. We ran about four or five different sugar bushes and had to haul sap and wood quite a ways. Brother Andy would load the trailer up with slabs at the sawmill and head for the sugar house. He had to go down Rt#422, a four-lane highway, and Andy was a little crazy anyway with a wheel in his hand. That day he lost the muffler on the tractor and he was roaring down 422 with a load of slabs as fast as that tractor could go. A state cop pulled him over and gave him a warning. We sure got a laugh out of that, but Leon was mad at the cop.

    One day when Leon was gone, I told the boys that if we take that tractor out on the road and put it out of gear and put the trailer in high gear, it'll be just like a car. We almost wrecked that day. We would have been alright if that tractor would have had springs like a car. When those front wheels started bouncing off the road where it had cradle knolls it was time to scrap that idea. We were glad to get that baby stopped. Now Chalker's stationary sawmill was inside a good building, but not very big. There was a 6-cylinder greyhound bus motor upstairs. The belts came down through the floor. Also, the throttle came down right where the sawyer stood. This was a left-handed Enterprise mill with a friction feed and the old Enterprise dogs. These mills weren't built for speed. Either that or I wasn't. The first day I sawed I swiped the big back door off the wall. Everything was back-ackwards. But anyway, we sawed quite a bit of lumber on it.

    This was about 46 years ago but I remember I sawed some lumber on that mill that I'll never forget. I'm still ashamed of myself. They were 2by5by24' long out of little fresh-cut soft maple logs. They were everything but 2by5. If I would have seen Uncle Erp Miller or Freeman Yoder walk in, I would have run for the woods. Freeman would still be laughing. One time I was sawing, and brother Smiley was off bearing. The lumber all had to be carried out the door and piled outside. This one-day 3by3by9's. I was slicing them off three at a time. I cut off 5 and Smiley was out the door and I seen they were leaning into the saw. There was just a little round splitter on the husk. When I saw that, I threw myself on the floor and none too quick as the pieces started to fly. I crawled out the side door on my hands and knees. Don't ever believe a man can 't run on hands and knees. Bangety, crashety bang. Smiley came tearing in there thinking old Dan was dead. I was outside the side door without a mark on me. There were pieces of 3by5 all over that building. Now, when I think back, I just have to shiver.

One time Lester Hostetler's Elmer was off bearing for me. And we decided to bachelor a week at a time. We stayed in Chalker's old milk house. There was a nice couch and an army cot to sleep on. Lester claimed the couch and I didn't care because at that time I could sleep anywhere. Well, the first night at 1:30 in the morn there was an awful commotion. Lester had the wastebasket and was banging at something on the floor. I don't know what language he was talking, but it was all garbled up. A bumble bee had stung him on the hand. So he didn't get to bed the rest of the night. The next day his hand was swelled so bad we couldn't work. We carried that couch outside the next morning and we went real easy. When we got it outside there was this cloth covering the back. Lester tore it off real easy and there was a big bumblebee nest. I'll never forget how big that queen bee was.

The man that owned the sugar bush where they boiled sap was named Big John and he was big. I'll never forget, he had elephantitus in one leg and that leg was big. I think he got it in the war. Another man I remember was named Paul. He used to fly with Leon. Paul went to another state one time and flew a plane home for his buddy. Before he got home, he got an oil leak in the engine and black oil splattered all over his windshield. Paul stuck his head out the window and tried to land in a field. He came in too low and his landing gear caught the electric wires and flipped the plane on its back in the field. It caught fire and burned up, but Paul got out. He was just as crazy to fly after that as he was before.

Chapter 19

This chapter will be about some of our good friends. We'll start with Jerry and Alice Jackson. Alice is the girl I wrote about in my other book. She was a pretty single girl when we moved out here. Then she started running with one of the Jackson boys and before long she was Mrs. Jerry Jackson. Now, Jerry was a chocolate fudge expert. He could make the best fudge money could buy. When he was in Vietnam, he made fudge over there. I'm getting ahead of my story a little bit. Alice is still a pretty girl, but like the rest of us, years and miles are starting to show a bit. Jerry came home from the Army and him and Alice got married. A while after they were married, Jerry said one night he wanted some fudge. So Alice got her pans, chocolate, thermometer, and everything ready and she start making fudge. She measured everything very carefully and that's something Jerry never did. He just slapped things together and, bingo, he had fudge. Alice dibbled and dabbled around, and Jerry went out to the kitchen and she had the candy thermometer in the fudge. I guess Jerry said when's the fudge ready. She said don't get in a hurry. Well, Jerry put cold water in the fudge and that stuff set up and couldn't even get it out of the pan. Now, this was years ago, and Jerry said she hasn't made him any fudge since. Must be Alice's motto is, if at first, you don't succeed, quit. Now if a man does something and it doesn't turn out right, he tries a little harder and a little harder till he gets it right.

Years ago, Mat baked a pie. I don't remember what it was, but I griped about something and it was several years till I got another pie and that's the truth. So, from then on hard crusts, soggy crusts, filling not enough sugar in it, it didn't matter what, I ate it and shut up. And can that girl bake pies now. But I think for Jerry's sake Alice should take another stab at making fudge.

For Christmas, I got quite a few gifts. Among them was a big black rubber spider, a rubber octopus, and a rubber bullfrog. I already had a rubber rat. Some of these women have no sense of humor. No.1, they should know with three feet of snow outside, there won't be any spiders running around. Have I had fun with that spider? All the kicking, screeching, and stomping around, my brother Andy would just enjoy it all. I think people are glad to see me come sometimes and also glad to see me go again. I don't go away very much, but the other afternoon (Sunday) we were over by Uncle Chubby's widow, Lydia. I took my playthings along and did we have fun. When we were leaving, I heard one of the girls remark about leaving my rubber zoo at home next time. My brother Andy got me started scaring people and it got to a kind of a hobby.

Jan.31,2004. A cold snowy month it has been It's been a year now since they cut me all up. The cold weather is hard on me. I'm out in my little workshop every day. I missed two days in Jan. I quit taking some more dope six days ago. I'm off of almost everything. But I feel bad. I feel like I don't have a friend in this big wide world, and that's not a nice feeling. The doctors give you this stuff to get you over the hump but when you quit taking it, it gets pretty rough. But what would we do without it?

Abe C. Miller's widow died last week with cancer. That was hard on me. I'm still not over it. She lived tight in back of us. Me and Mom have been married for over 40 years and it sure doesn't seem that long. Mom was always there when I needed her, and we've had a good marriage. God must have known I needed a woman like that. I told my boys already if I'd have married a mean old dame, we would have had only one fight and it would still be going. So anyway, let's go to another chapter.

Chapter 20

When I was scaling lumber at Spartywood, I had a piler named Kile. One day we were working away and Kile asked, where can I buy some baby rabbits.

I said, "Kile, what do you want with baby rabbits."

He said, " I have a pet snake. It's a Burmese python. It was either 11 or 15ft long."

I said," Kile, what in the world do you want a pet like that for. "

He said, "Hey, some people have dogs and some have cats, but myself, I like snakes."

I said, "Do you sleep in the same house as that snake?"

He said, "Yeah, but it's in a pen."

That gave me the shivers. Imagine sleeping and waking up with that slimy thing under the covers with you, touching your bare skin.

I said, "Kile, you have a problem."

He said," Yeah, I need some baby rabbits."

I said, "What for?"

He said, "To feed my snake. I put the rabbit in the cage, and it knows. It runs back and forth, going nuts and the snake watches it. When it gets in the right place, THUNK. He's got him and eats him whole."

I said, "Kile, If I had a rabbit, you wouldn't buy them."

He said he'll bring it out to my place someday. I said if I tell him not to come any closer, he'd better stop because I'd use the shotgun on it. He said don't do that and I said he'd better stop. One night son Tobe was here. He was tied up at the hitching rail when this car pulled in and two guys got out. The one opened the back door and started pulling something out. Tobe was headed for the hitching Tail and untied his horse and headed for home. He does not like snakes. Well, Kile pulled this big thing out of the car and hung it around his neck. It was wrapped around his leg and his belly.

He started walking across the yard towards me and I said "That's far enough.

He stopped and said, "Don't you want to pet it?"

I said," No, I don't want to pet it."

If I had something like that living in my house, I'd be a bundle of nerves.

Kile came to work a few weeks after that and said his snake got loose. He looked for it for 2 or 3 days. Then He heard his neighbor's Siamese cat came up missing. So, he went over, and they started looking around and they found Kile's snake in her basement and it had swallowed her cat. She was one mad woman, and I can't blame her. So Kile was running all overlooking for another Siamese cat.

Chapter 21

I used to say I'd about as soon mess my pants as get wet, but last spring I kind of changed my mind. I was taking radiation treatments and every week I was losing two lbs. This one nurse weighed me once a week. Finally, she really got on me.

She said, "You don't have any more to lose."

I tried telling her, "I couldn't eat very well."

She said to take more Boost through my feeding tube.

O.K. I Started taking another can a day. The 2nd day I was out in my little workshop piddling around I couldn't do much. I still used my cane to walk. I started to get a belly ache. I mean a big bellyache. I thought, oh my, I'm not going to make it to the hisley. I crossed my legs and held my cheeks together with both hands, but it was no use. It ran down both my legs right into my shoes. There I was, I couldn't holler, I didn't know where Mom was or the water hose. So, I got my cane and waddled towards the house. Oh, my what a feeling, I started banging on the outhouse with my cane. Bang, bang, bang. Then the chicken house door flew open, and Mom asked what's wrong. I motioned her over and pulled up my pant leg and showed her what was wrong. Oh my, what a mess. Well, Mom was jabbering away at me and I wasn't even listening. I had my mind on a little nurse. I was finally cleaned up again. I was in a hurry to get cleaned up again, but I thought, what's the hurry, you're not going anywhere.

The next day I had to go to the Franklin Hospital for another radiation treatment. I went looking for a little nurse. I finally found her, and I said on account of you I shit myself.

Oh, you had a loose bowel movement, she said.

I said, "Yeah, all on account of you."

We had a nice little conversation about this with me doing most of the talking, of course. But I quit taking more Boost. Must be some of my doctors heard about it because the next week when I went to get weighed, she said," Mr. Byler, you gained some weight."

But one of my doctors was standing there and he had his foot on the scales.

At the time I was talking with my little helper. This thing, you stick a tube in your mouth and press a button and make your lips go, and form the words and this thing would talk, but was hard to understand. I didn't know if she understood what I said, but she told my wife, boy did I get it, so she understood a little.

I remember when I was just a kid. We lived in Bundysburg. Dad walked home from Grandads and he came across lots. He was almost home when he had to go. He thought he could make it, but he had to crawl through the fence, and he got caught. He'd pull a bit and then he'd poop a little bit and so on. By the time he got home, he was a mess.

Chapter 22

Now let's go hunting again. There's getting to be quite a few bears around here.

They took a piece of timber off in back of the place where I live. The log cutter said from the tracks and signs he's seen, there's 7 different bears in this block. A couple of years ago, it was in the spring, but still had snow on the ground, one morning Mom saw this deer going up the road with his tongue hanging out. He was slipping and sliding, trying to go faster. The man that lived across the road from us happened to be looking and he saw it all. There was a bear after this deer and when the deer hit the road the bear stopped and turned around and went the other way.

One morning I was in the outhouse doing my duty and a couple of times I heard something outside, and I thought it was Mom. Finally, I came out and stood looking around and son Ervin came over from across the road and said, "Did you see that big bear come out of your driveway." He said it was a big one. That's probably, what I heard when I was doing my duty. Now if I would have opened that door and come face to face with that bear, I would have needed more toilet paper.

It was going towards fall and son Dennis was hard up so he decided he'd get a deer with the bow. He said he's gonna try and get some meat. About 45 min later he came out of the drive really hoofing it. I said, where's the deer.

He said, "Hey, I'm hard up and all but I'm not hunting back there tonight."

He had bumped into a big bear. He went one way and the bear probably went the other way.

I used to sharpen bands for a man in Cherry Tree named Bob Lesh. Bob was in the pallet business. His place bordered a big game land. This is about 20 miles from our place. He said they dump a lot of bears there that are pests or make trouble other places. They trap them and dump them out next to Bob's place. In the summer on nice evenings,

Bob would sit outside with a bottle of honey and a .357 mag., fully loaded. There was a creek just below Bob's yard and in the hot summer, sometimes the bear would lay in the creek to cool off. Sometimes they'd come right up to Bob's yard and he'd hold the honey in one hand and the gun in the other hand in case a bear got nasty.

One night Bob and his son were sitting there, Bob's son had the honey and Bob had the gun. This big bear walked into the yard and walked right up to them. He started licking honey out of the jar. When the honey was all gone the bear just stood there and looked at them. Then he reached over and took ahold of his boy's leg. Not hard. He backhanded him across the face. And did that bear explode! He took a swipe at Bob's boy, but he went back in his chair and the bear missed him. Then he turned around and trundled off to the woods.

He told his boy, "Don't you ever do that again."

He said, "Hey, that was my leg."

He told me that bear will never know how near came to being dead. Bob came home one night after dark and pulled up to his house. There laid a big bear on his porch. He blew the horn and hollered at him, but he didn't move. He had to go get help to chase it off before he could get in his own house. Now I have a 410 that would have changed that bear's mind real quick.

I know of a guy, I'm not going to put his name in here. He had a big dog and one night that dog was howling and howling. He got up and flashed out there and his big dog was backed up as far as his chain would let him, and a bear was eating his dog food out of his dish. He chased him off but the next night he was back, so he got the old 12-guage out and kerboom. He said you should have seen the dust fly when that shot hit him. But he still kept coming back.

I have a good friend that lives on Hatchtown Road just below where I live. Milliron is his name. He's a taxidermist. Several years ago, he was bow hunting in the back of our place. He was way up in a tree watching for deer. Here comes this big bear and he tracked him right up to his tree. When Milliron got into this tree, he had to jump to grab the bottom limb. This bear came up to this tree and stood up. He was so big his chin was on top of this limb. Then he started climbing up this tree. Milliron didn't want to shoot him, but he didn't know what to do. Then he happened to think he had a chew of snuff in his mouth so he started spitting snuff juice. Finally, he hit the bear in the eye. The bear got mad, but he stopped. Then he started climbing again and he kept spitting and hit him in the eye again, and he stopped again. Finally, the bear crawled down and left. When he was out of sight Milliron got down and he also left, I don't blame him.

    Milliron was bow hunting in Bob Morris' backfield, that's also in the block we live in, where he saw this animal out in the field. He was up in a tree a little in the woods. It was brushy but he could see the field pretty good, he had his movie camera with him. Finally, it got close enough that he could see it was a bobcat hunting mice. He tried to get it on his movie camera, but it was too brushy. I've seen one bobcat since we live out here so you don't see them very often.

    I like to chuck field on the back 40. I had a 50-gallon barrel for a lawn chair and a cushion for a gun rest for my 30-30. A deadly combination if I must say so myself. People laugh at my 30-30 but they do not realize what a killer it is. Now, for several years after my brain surgery, I just wasn't doing so good. Things were just different. So, I spent time in the backfield hunting chucks. Before this, I had heard of people seeing coyotes. Well, the way the game commission is, who knows, I talked to people who knew coyotes and found out their favorite breakfast is a Woodpecker, and their favorite dinner is a house cat.

    So, this one day I was in the backfield hunting chucks. I had 4-power glasses. I kept glassing the field. It was over 300 yd to the bottom end. The field was freshly mowed. All at once, I saw something stretched out in the weeds right beside where it was mowed. I looked and looked, but I couldn't make it out. I had my 225 Model 7 Rem with a 6-24 power scope on it, but I was so shook up, I forgot all about it. I only had 4 shells for the 223. I knew I could get lead into it, whatever it was, but a 223 isn't a very big gun and just four shells, no, I don't think so. I sat watching this thing, trying to figure out what this thing was. This field has woods on all four sides. All at once, a white cat came out of the woods on the right edge of the field, about 50 yards from the bottom end.

It was hunting mice, heading towards whatever lay there. The cat got so close then all at once it stopped, head up in the air as if it smelled something. It ran up towards me about 100 yds then started hunting again. Now I knew it was there somewhere and I only had four shells. I've got good guns but sometimes in tight situations, these guns get a little nervous and don't want to hold still. I can't run anymore, and I didn't think I could climb a tree and there was only one thing left and that was, get out of there. And get I did. Just hoping Joe Cicatella or Ronny Sellon didn't find out about it. I didn't feel good that day, but this bugged me. I told mom about the white cat and she said there's one hanging around here.

The next forenoon I loaded my 30-30. strapped my shell belt on and I was loaded for bear. I headed for the backfield, I couldn't walk fast, just took my good old time. I made a circle around the field and started back the way that white cat was headed. All at once, I came on a ball of white hair. That's all. No fur, no bones, nothing but this ball of hair about 6" in diameter. I walked home again and told Mom, come on, we're going for a walk. I took her back to the field and showed her that white hair and said, what is that. She said that's what's left of that white cat. Now, whatever that was could see me and I couldn't see it so I'll never know.

Chapter 23

Now Lester Byler "Dog Patch," wrote a book and he wrote in there about me and Pinky and how we were afraid of horses and all that. Pinky drove an outlaw for several years. I still remember her name, Mable. She was more outlaw than horse. She'd kick, run away and several other things and Pinky drove her in the buggy and worked her in the team. So, I know that's not so about Pinky.

Now myself, when I was young and in my prime my old Daddy sold horses for Harold Dixon. We lived in Parkman at the time. Dad would get seven or eight horses at a time. Me and brother Andy would hook them in the buggy for the first time as they just got off the track. I told Harold I want a little bay pacer and he said he'd keep his eyes open. One night I came home from work and Mom said Harold was here and unloaded a little horse and him and Dad went somewhere. So, me and Andy headed for the barn. I thought she was awful jumpy. But we finally got her harnessed. Had a time putting the bridle on, but finally had her ready to hook up. Now the fun really started. It took us quite a while, but we finally had her hooked up. Andy had her by the head, and I jumped on the buggy and I said turn her loose.

Did I get a surprise, I went around in circles so fast, I was hollering, "Whoa, whoa.!"

I didn't have any control with the lines at all. Andy finally grabbed her by the head and got her stopped. We put her in the barn and unharnessed her and I sat down to wait for Harold Dixon. Harold and Dad finally came home.

I asked Harold, "What do you think you're doing, bringing me an outlaw like that."

He said what happened and we told him and did he laugh. He picked that horse in Crawford and was taking him to some Burkholder to break. That horse had never been messed with.

My dad was a horse trader. He got a horse once, it was a good horse, safe, went down the road not afraid of anything, but once in a while he would lay his ears back and pinch his tail in but he never kicked. We were all at my brother Jake's place on Swine creek road one day and Dad said to Andy, put your open bridle on my horse and hook him in your buggy. I helped Andy hook up and jumped on the buggy with him.

That horse walked out the driveway so unconcerned, I thought, a piece of cake. Then Bam, splinters were flying and there was a hole in the dashboard. That horse took off like he was jet-powered and kicking with every jump. We were in one ditch, almost tipping over, then in the other ditch. The boys said Dad was standing in the middle of the road watching and every time we'd almost tip over, he would lean way sideways to try and keep us from tipping over. Then he headed for the house and said, Mom, give me a nerve pill.

We were flying around side the buggy and I was trying to get ahold of one line. I finally got ahold of the left line. Then we really put the pressure on then the bit broke in half. Then we went buggy riding. We hit one mailbox and were headed for downtown Bundysburg. Us boys were mostly raised in Bundysburg and we knew there was a sinkhole in this one ditch. All we had to steer with was the bridle leather across his nose. We started a little way before we got there and it worked. I told Andy, that's the only chance we have. That horse hit that sinkhole and went in up to his belly. He couldn't move. I remember Andy was so glad to get off that buggy, he just made one leap and landed on his belly. We pot him unhitched, pulled the buggy back, and finally got the horse out on the road. His back legs were a mess, bloody and swelled up.

Well, here comes little bow-legged Dad down the road, walking a pretty good clip. He asked what happened and we told him. He said you should have shot him right there. He thought a little bit, then said, well he's broke now, let's take him back and hitch him in my buggy. I said, no, Dad," I'll never get on that buggy with that horse again." We took Mom and Dad home that night. That horse was ruined. I don't know why Dad didn't have that horse reined up that day, he must have really trusted that horse. Usually, he just reined a horse up. He never put kicking straps on a horse.

Dad was an old horse trader. He never asked anybody how old a horse was, he just looked at his teeth. One time, I was just five or six, Dad had a good buggy horse. Mom told him one morning we have almost nothing in the house to eat, the rent was due (which was 5:00 a month) and we have no money. After breakfast, Dad hooked his horse up and didn't come home till that night. He'd traded horses five times and came home with the same horse and had $50.00 in his pocket. $50.00 was a lot of money in those days.

Another thing I remember, I can't remember whose funeral it was, but Dad and Mom and baby Smiley and Andy Mast's Mary went to the funeral. Coming home, coming down Townline hill, his horse started kicking and running away. He hung on and tried to control him but couldn't. The horse kicked loose from the buggy, Dad had ahold of the lines so tight and he hung on. It picked him off the seat and over the dashboard and he landed on his feet on the road. It ripped both heels off his shoes and he couldn't walk for a couple of days.

Another horse Dad had; he came down Tucker Hill one day. Tucker Hill is a steep hill with 3 curves in it. He started down the hill and that horse started kicking and kicked all the way down to the bottom. When he got her stopped, she had both hind feet over the crosspiece. He unhooked her, turned the buggy around, and hooked her up again. He always had a good whip on the buggy. He went up Tucker Hill as fast as she could go, beating her with every jump. When they got to the top he turned around and he said that time she knew how to go down the hill.

Now I'll have to confess some of my horse sense. I was scaling lumber at Brush Run Lumber when son-in-law Toby Kuhns pulled in with a horse and cart.

Toby said, "I've found a good horse for you."

I owned five buggy horses at the time for me and the boys. I bought the boy's horses but never paid any attention to them. So, I laid my stick, pencil, and tally book on the pile and jumped on the cart and went for a ride. Nice horse, nice pacer, a good horse, you could just tell. We got back to the mill and I wanted to get back to work so I said, how much, Tobe. I got my checkbook out and was ready to write him a check when he started laughing and said, this is your horse. It's the one your son Tobe drives.

I said, "Tobe, if you'd have pulled this off, you'd have paid dearly."

Another time church was just 3/4 mile down the road. The boys walked but I told Mom I'm going to hook up Imp and drive. Well, we got on the road, Imp had her head up and wanted to go. I said what's the matter with her this morning. Mom said this isn't our horse. Now sometimes Mom would come up with some crazy stuff and this was one of them.

I said, "I don't want to hear it. Don't you think I know which is our horse?"

We got to church, and I was telling some of the men I don't know what's the matter with my old mare was this morning, I had to hang on all the way down this morn. Going home it was the same thing. Mom said again, this isn't our horse. I just ignored her. We got home and unhooked and Mom said, pick up that horse's tail. I did and it was a single barrel, one of the boy's horses. Oh well, we can't be right all the time.

I remember when we lived in Bundysburg before we moved to Sparty, I opened the barn door one morning and I had a barn full of cats. They had Jitter written all over them. I've had pony teams almost all my married life, some good and some bad. I had one good pony, I thought, and I bought another one in Bristolville, Ohio. A nice pony. I put five kids on his back and led him all around the and he was just like a little lamb. One night Dad and Mom were at our place and I told Dad, let's hook that new pony up with my other one.

He said, "O.K."

I harnessed them up and we took them across the road to Abe V Byler's backfield where I had my sled. We hooked them to the sled and Dad had the lines. He said he'll take them the first round. He told them to go, and that new pony went nuts. He jumped off the sled and got them stopped.

He said, "If that was my horse, I'd shoot him right between the eyes."

Now, Dad always liked to run my stuff down and that didn't hit me just right. I said, give me those lines, you can't drive horses anyway! I shouldn't have said that as I paid dear for that remark.

I jumped on the sled and said, "GIDDAP!"

Famous last words. Those ponies took off and there was no stopping them. I sat down on the sled and tried to stop them, then we hit a furrow kind of katty wampus and it flipped the sled then they were dragging me on my belly, still picking up speed, or so it seemed. And there was only one thing to do and that was let them fly. And that is what I did. There was a new three-strand barbed wire fence around that field and I just knew they were going to try to go through it. They went down over the hill, out of sight and all at once, screech, I heard wire screech. I didn't know what I'd find but it was a mess. The ponies were both on their backs all tangled up with wire and harness leather, what a mess. I got them up and everything patched up, then came the hard part. I had to go face Dad. With me, Dad was one of those I told you so guys. So, I just had to eat crow and like it.

Several years ago, I bought a mare off of Lester "Dog Patch" son-in-law. She was pretty poor when I bought her but she started picking up weight. The more weight she gained the faster she could go. Joe down at the store has horses on the racetrack and he said, get me her tattoo number. I did and her name was Winsome Cobra I got her in good shape, and I couldn't handle her anymore. When I had her, old Lester wasn't doing much bragging about his horses. I think he was just a bit afraid, but he'd never admit it.

Chapter 24

Received a letter from Monon, Indiana today from a veterinary clinic. And I thought, what is going on here. I looked at the signature, Hites. That brought back a lot of memories in a hurry, My Dad used to cut logs for Carl Hites when I was just a boy. Carl was a good man to work for. That's where I got hooked on caterpillar saw-mill motors. That was the first one I'd sawed with. I remember Carl bought a new Mack lumber truck, a single axle. I think Clyde "Speedy" Roland was the truck driver. We moved the mill to another woods. The first load Speedy drove out to a place that was pretty slanted. He stopped the truck and got out. He told Carl he wouldn't drive that truck over that spot. He did and it rolled over. I'll never forget that Dad brought a bulldog home.

Another thing I remember about that truck, every time you'd get stuck, you'd twist an axle off. James Ketchum worked for Carl for a long time. He had a dog, but I can't remember his name. James had a Jeep pickup and when we'd move mill, he'd haul that cat motor in his pickup and he had a load. Carl bought two fence rows of solid Pin Oak, nice trees but rough. Dad wouldn't cut it. I was 14 years old, but I had a good teacher. Carl hired me a helper, a colored man, name of Jake Walker. Jake made a little of that block and tackle whiskey. Take a drink, walk a block and tackle anything. Jake was a good worker and I liked Jake. Rex Galey skidded logs, I can't remember who worked on the mill. Those were the good old days. I tell my boys about those brushy Pin Oak and they just kind of stare off into space as much as to say, "Yeah the old man is making it worse than it really was."

But you'd go out in the morning and uncover the slab fire ashes and you'd have instant heat, cook on one side and freeze on the other. Another thing, you would get a day off once in a while when it rained.

Set up stationary, you just keep working. Lewie Hites had a hunting camp in back of his farm somewhere. One night the Hite's boys were going to have a chicken supper back at the camp. It started getting dark and the boys told Lewie, go back and get the stove fired up and we'll get the chickens. So Lewie took off for camp and the boys went into Lewie's chicken house and got the chickens. Here Lewie was eating his own chickens and didn't know it. These were Lewie's brothers Bob, Ed, and Frank. I remember when Lewis was in the lumber business, he used to tell his sawyers he didn't care how thick they slabbed, as long as they could run them through the blower. Another thing he used to say was that if a 4by4 didn't roll off the truck, it didn't have too much bark on it. That was back in the good old days when there was only steel mill blocking.

Chapter 25

I sit in our little house this winter and dream of one more deer hunt. Maybe all an old deer hunter can do is dream. I'm thinking this summer, if I stay healthy, of building me a 7'by 10' hunting shanty with a bunk to lay down and sliding windows all around. I'd build it on skids, son John has a big team, and I wouldn't have to be far from the buildings. I have a brand-new stainless steel 30-30 marlin lever action deer rifle that's never been shot. I'll probably try it out on chucks this summer. I think it's about time me and Joe Cicatella and Tony Rose started stirring around again. It's been several years that we didn't hunt together. I still haven't forgotten that one big woodchuck. Probably. the biggest one I've ever seen. Joe was parked back in a field and I was standing on the back of the pickup leaning on the cab. I had my cushion to rest my gun on. All at once, this chuck stood up. She wasn't 100 yards from me and she was wide. She had her back turned towards me. I thought, grandmaw, you got old by being smart or lucky, or both, but that's gonna end right now. I thought to myself, she isn't even gonna know what hit her. Boom, and away she went. She didn't know what almost hit her. I think I did one of Tony's Indian war dances, but it didn't last long. I'll never know what happened, I was so sure of that shot. Spoiled my whole night, missing the chuck and watching Joe trying to hide those smiles.

I had another hunting buddy that's dead and gone now, Dick Drake. we were about the same age. One night we were chuck hunting in this big field, 500-yard shot. There was a shooting bench there and Dick had his sandbags along. I had my Model 7 rem. in a 223 cal with a 6-24 power scope on it. I set down at the bench first and started watching. This chuck stood up and she was a long way out. There was a breeze blowing from the side and I tried to allow for this and the way I had it sited in, I held just a tad high. She was out 400 yds. plus. I shot and she ducked. She stood up again and ducked again. I waited and she stood up again, Boom, I hit her in the same place. Dick said, let me have that bench. Dick had a Russian P C B, he couldn't even buy shells for it, he had to load his own. But it was his pet rifle. He also had a 6-24 scope on it with a rangefinder. He sat down, I think he set his rangefinder at 450 yards and boom, there was a dead chuck.

I said, "Well I'm not going to be able to stand you for the rest of the night."

But anyway, you don't win them all. You win a few you lose a few.

Billy Alma needs to be taken down a few notches again. I've been hearing little rumors about her. The latest I heard; Billy wanted popcorn one night with butter on it. And she wouldn't make it for him. Now if a man wants popcorn with butter on it the woman ought to make it for him. Not give him a song and dance about it. Joe will just have to give her another firecracker treatment this summer.

Several years ago, me and Joe were chuck hunting and we went past Monty's Ray's place. Ray's boys and son-in-laws were all home that day. Well, Joe had the big ones that day, 1/4 stick of dynamite. All the men were laying out in the yard that day. We were just going slow, and Joe got a big one out and lit it himself and threw it in the ditch. Ka-whoom, that thing went off. I looked back and everybody was on his feet. Just looked like that blast picked them right off the ground.

Another thing that happened one night that I got blamed for that I was innocent of. A lot of the children were still home, and I think Clara, the troublemaker started it all. We had a big living room with chairs all around it. There was a register in the ceiling to heat the upstairs. There was an easy chair under the register. It didn't matter if it was a complete stranger, if somebody sat in that chair, that girl would pour water down on their head. Some of those people woke up in a hurry. Well, I was telling Joe about this and right away he thought of something. We decided on a night to go chuck hunting, me, Joe, and Tony. Now Joe said, have kids in all the chairs but two.

He said, you come out and say, "Joe, I'm not quite ready yet, come on in."

So, Joe and Tony came in and Joe took his cap off and motioned Tony to do the same. Tony thought what's the matter with him, I've been in Cider Dan's house before and I never took my cap off, but he did. Joe took the rocking chair by the stove and Tony sat in the easy chair under the register.

Tony said, "Boy I could sit in this chair all day."

About then he let out a yip and said, "What the heck?"

By then Joe burst out laughing. And I got the blame for it all. I tried to tell Tony it was all Joe's fault.

But he said, "Listen, Cider, it was your house so don't blame it on Joe."

I said, "Joe planned it all."

He said, "It was your house, so don't blame it on somebody else."

So, life goes on.

Several years ago, I was hunting chucks in the backfield, I had my lawn chair, my 55-gal barrel and my cushion, and the old faithful 30-50. I told Mom I'd be gone about two hours. It was going towards fall and that's my favorite time of year. I think I had two chucks and time kind of got away from me.

Now if I'd listen to Mom, I'd be one of the biggest outlaws around. She says God put Deer, turkeys, rabbits, etc. on this earth to eat and she sees nothing with shooting them, no matter what time of the year. She's right, but we have game laws we should try to obey most of the time. I have nothing against a poor man getting a little meat on the side, or a farmer. As long as I don't have to pay the fine, I could care less.

Well, anyway, I was sitting there when down at the lower end of the field these black started coming out of the brush. I grabbed my spotting scope, turkeys. And a big flock. They started feeding up towards me. I just sat there and watched, trigger finger feeling a little funny if you know what I mean. There were several gobblers and one big one. I had the post on my rifle scope right on the spot where his neck fastens on his body. But I knew if I shot, there'd be somebody back there watching. So, I just sat and watched. They came within 80 yds. of me. The gobbler kept watching me, but I didn't move. Then they started feeding over towards the brush and finally went into the brush.

Somebody behind me said, "Why didn't you shoot."

I jumped and whirled around, and it was my wife. She got worried and came looking for me. I told her I knew if I shot, there'd be somebody back there watching, and my feeling was right.

Fri. Feb.27, 2004 I've been sick all week and I mean sick. I've lain in the house almost all week and that's not me. When the kids were little, I worked a lot of sick days, but anymore I just can't seem to get it together. I guess I could go to a doctor. You know, I like doctors, I just don't like going to them. Seems like when you've had cancer, they're always probing and trying to find something that isn't there. I guess that's their job, but I still don't have to like it. I've found out one thing this winter, the cold air and that hole in my throat don't get along. I think I've had an infection in my lungs for about a month. The stuff I Cough up is horrible. And you cough it out of that hole in your throat. Am always afraid of it plugging up. It is getting better, but slow. I blame it on those 36 radiation treatments I had. Once you've had radiation, your immune system is ka-put. And so life goes on.

Chapter 26

Now my mind goes back to our young married years and some of the rat-infested places we lived in. One place that was bad was the house beside Roman Troyer on Rt#88. Oh, those were the good old days, and we didn't know it. This was a well-built house, but nobody lived in it for a while. Rueben Swartz bought this place on a land contract before we lived there, for $75.99 a month, and that was a steep payment in those days. In fine print that Rueben didn't see, it said in two years the owner could demand the rest of his money. The guy demanded his money and Rueben tried his best to borrow the rest of it, but he didn't have enough paid for a down payment and couldn't borrow it, so he lost it. I'll never forget that. That fixed me on land contract.

We moved in the house. A couple of windows were broke but we didn't think anything of it, but a couple of nights later we found out. When 10 o'clock came, it was time for bed because here come the rats. Now, I don't like a mouse I don't like a snake, but I hate a rat. We set poison, traps, but there were so many of them. One Friday night sister Sarah and brother Smiley came down and were going to stay overnight.

We were all playing cards and I told them, "10:00, we'll have to go to bed as the rats will take over."

Well, at almost 10:00 here comes the first rat. Sarah wouldn't sleep at our place and went over to Roman Troyer's to sleep, Smiley slept on the couch. We weren't in bed long, something flew across the floor, then everything was quiet.

Pretty soon I heard," Hey", pretty loud.

I said," What's the matter out there. "

He said the rats are trying to get on the couch with me.

We didn't live there long. We also lived way back in off RT 88 below Harvey Moss. Dennis was the baby and one night me and Mattie woke up the same time. Something hit the floor with a thud. Mat shut the bedroom door right away and I jumped up on the bed. I made up my mind, rat, you jump on this bed, you can have the bedroom, bed, and the whole nine yards because I'm leaving.

We had a little rat terrier house dog. Mom opened the bedroom door and called her and she was right there. And then the fun started. Around and around the bedroom went the rat and the dog. The rat was shrieking, the dog barking and I was standing on the bed, taking it all in. Mom was trying to help the dog, and all at once, the rat disappeared.

We couldn't figure out where she went. Mom started opening dresser drawers and out she popped. The dog finally caught her and put an end to her.

Mom chased one out the driveway once, swinging a broom. She got her before she got on the road.

I have very good memories of good old Parkman, Ohio. I remember when zoning went in and everybody was in an uproar. Elmer Weaver was putting an addition on his house when one of those zoning guys stopped in.

Elmer was on a ladder and the guy said," Do you have a building permit?"

Elmer said, "Yes I do and it's hanging on my wall and it cost $79.95 and it's a 30-30 Winchester and it's about the best building permit you can get."

The guy up and left and never did come back.

Now all that's left of the Parkman Church, that still lives there is Roman Troyer's widow (Mat) Mose Troyer's widow(Jemima, and Elmer Weaver and his wife, Em. We played ball for 2 years in Mastville. I probably can't name them all but was Mahlon Mast's Alton and Clarence (Moose), Roman Troyer (Balogna Bender). I don't know where he ever got that nickname. Mose Troyer, Poor Dave's Al, Levi's Al. Johnny Mast was the other team's relief pitcher. think Al's Mart played. I played left field. I just can't think of any others, but I know there were a lot more that played because we had two teams.

Dad and Mom lived in Mastville for quite a while. One night we were at Dad's and some of the neighbors were there. It was pitch dark that night, summertime. Finally, old Alvin Mast started for home. He lived just across the road. All at once, crashety-bang. Then everything was quiet, then somebody hollered," What happened?"

Alvin said, "Oh I fell over the gal-danged wagon." One of the kids had left the wagon out there and Alvin fell over it. When we saw he wasn't hurt, we could laugh. He laughed right with us.

When I ride around Geauga County now, I just can't believe my eyes, the changes that were made in almost 37 years that we live in Sparty. Take the old Katie Jake farm on Rt# 87 and bordered on Townline road. This was a nice farm. Uncle Jake had Ayrshire cows with these big horns. Katie Jake's Bill cultivated corn and I walked behind the cultivator, and if he covered a stalk, I'd uncover it. I remember once in a while I ate there, and Aunt Katie can sure cook. One time we had mashed potatoes and smoked ham gravy, home-smoked ham, potato salad, peas, and pie.

Now, these were the days when we didn't have much at home to eat. And when I sat down to a meal like that, did I dig in. Mom used to say she was ashamed of us boys when we went anywhere for dinner. All us boys must have got more to eat than poor little Bim. He's still just a scrawny little guy, just never grew. Well, Bim, I'd rather be little and scrawny than the shape I'm in.

So, I think I'll bring this book to an end and if I ticked anybody off, that wasn't my intention and if I did, I'm sorry already. I don't think I have an enemy in this whole world and I sure hope not.

Come and visit me. I love company,

Cider Dan

Index of Names

Abe C. Miller's widow, 58
Allen, Brad, 42
Alma, Billy, 17, 75
Al's Mart, 79
AL's Mel, 11
Aul, Joe's son Aul, 2
Aunt Katie, 80
Barstow, Fred, 9
Big John, 56
Bimber, Guy, 15
Bristolville, Ohio, 70
Brush Run Lumber, 41, 69
Buell's Corner, 10
Buell's Gorner Store, 16
Burkholder, 67
Byler, Abe V., 70
Byler, Amelia, 45
Byler, Andy, 3, 33, 40, 55, 58, 67
Byler, Billy, 31
Byler, Bim, 1, 7, 13, 33, 47, 80
Byler, Clara, 41, 75
Byler, Dan, 47
Byler, Dan J., 48
Byler, Dennis, 25, 28, 40, 63
Byler, Ervin, 31, 63
Byler, Esther, 25
Byler, Ida, 33
Byler, Jake, 45
Byler, John, 25, 43
Byler, Lester, 67
Byler, Lester (Dog Patch), 71
Byler, Marty, 9

Byler, Mary, 9
Byler, Noah, 9, 13, 29, 45
Byler, Smiley, 69
Byler, Steve, 1
Byler, Tobe, 9, 59, 70
Byler,Tobe, 26
Carnation, 46
Chalker Lumber Co., 54
Cherry Tree, 63
Chubby Dan, 5
Chubby's John, 43
Chubby's Ben, 43
Cicatella, Joe, 16, 17, 25, 31, 38, 48, 66, 74, 75
Cider Dan, 75
Clintonville, 43
Coblentz, Dave, 21
Cox, Al, 32
Cripple Billy, 17, 41
Dixon, Harold, 67
Don, 12
Dragon, Dr., 35
Drake, Dick, 74
Franklin Hospital, 35, 61
Freeman, 2
Galey, Rex, 72
Geauga County, 80
Gibbs, Herby, 33
Gingerich, Mel, 43
Glo Ray Inc, 12
Hatchtown Road, 64
Henderson, Dr., 35
Hites, Carl, 72

Hites, Lewie, 72
Host, John, 50
Hostetler, Eli, 33
Jackson, Jerry and Alice, 57
Jakie, Cider Jake's, 15
Jitter, 12
Katie Jake farm, 80
Katie Jake's Bill, 80
Kaufman, Bishop Jake Kaufman, 2
Kemp, Jeff, 50
Kemp, Scotty, 50
Kile, 59
Kurtz, Joe, 2
Leon, 56
Leon's dad, 54
Lesh, Bob, 63
Lester Hostetle'r Elmer, 56
Levi's Al, 79
Lewie, Bob, Ed, and Frank, 73
Lincoln, Larry, 12
Lit Dan's Jerry, 6
Lit Dan's Mel, 6
Long, Dr., 52
Mahlon's Ben, 43
Mahlon's Eli, 43
Manas Troyer's Roy, 9
Martin, Dana, 38, 40
Maryann, 2
Mast, Alvin, 80
Mast, Johnny, 79
Mastville, 80
McManus, Pat, 29
Mespo, 35
Middlefield, 3
Mike John's Eli, 45
Miller, Abe C., 15
Miller, Al J., 6

Miller, Andy, 44
Miller, Bob and John, 44
Miller, Uncle Erp, 55
Milliron, 64
Monty's Ray's, 75
Mony's Andy, 19
Morris, Bob, 65
Moss, Harvey, 78
Nazzarro, Dr., 35
Nichols, Dick, 43
Old Pudge, 46
Parkman Church, 79
Parkman, Ohio, 79
Patchen, Hank, 20
Patterson, Don, 49
Paul, 56
Pinky, 5, 11, 67
Pirogos, Dr., 35
Poor Dave's Al, 79
Quinn's Market, 34
Reese, Bill, 23
Roland, Clyde, 72
Rose, John, 29
Rose, Mike, 29
Rose, Tony, 28, 74, 75
Roswell Cancer Institute, 37
Rufus, 7
Sawmill Dan, 3
Sellon, Ronny, 66
Slaubaugh, Ervin, 21
Slaubaugh, Joe, 41
Smiley, 55
Swartz, Rueben, 78
Swine Creek, 2
Tillery, Carol, 33
Tillery, Kenny, 33
Tony, Joe, 28
Troyer, Mose, 79

Troyer, Roman, 78, 79
Tucker Hill, 69
Uncle Ben's, 1
Uncle Chubby's widow, Lydia, 58
Vanderhoff, Buzzy, 47
Walker, Jake, 72

Weaver, Elmer and Em, 79
Whitey, 40, 41
Yoder, Elmer, 45
Yoder, Freeman, 55
Yogi, 2
Zook, Leonard, 37
Zook, Mary, 37

Made in United States
Orlando, FL
09 March 2022